ESSAYS IN MUSICA

ESSAYS IN
MUSICAL ANALYSIS

By

DONALD FRANCIS TOVEY

CONTENTS

ESSAYS IN
MUSICAL ANALYSIS

By
DONALD FRANCIS TOVEY

Volume VI
SUPPLEMENTARY ESSAYS
GLOSSARY AND INDEX

LONDON
OXFORD UNIVERSITY PRESS

Oxford University Press, Ely House, London W. 1

GLASGOW NEW YORK TORONTO MELBOURNE WELLINGTON
CAPE TOWN IBADAN NAIROBI DAR ES SALAAM LUSAKA ADDIS ABABA
DELHI BOMBAY CALCUTTA MADRAS KARACHI LAHORE DACCA
KUALA LUMPUR SINGAPORE HONG KONG TOKYO

First Published 1939
Tenth Impression 1972

PRINTED IN GREAT BRITAIN
AT THE UNIVERSITY PRESS, OXFORD
BY VIVIAN RIDLER
PRINTER TO THE UNIVERSITY

CONTENTS

BACH

CARL PHILIPP EMANUEL BACH

GLUCK

MOZART

BEETHOVEN

MÉHUL

MENDELSSOHN

SCHUMANN

WAGNER

BACH

CCXXIII. OVERTURE IN C MAJOR, FOR ORCHESTRA

1 (*Grave: leading to Allegro*). 2 *Courante*. 3 *Gavotte I and II*. 4 *Forlane*.
5 *Menuet I and II*. 6 *Bourrée I and II*. 7 *Passepied I and II*.

Of Bach's four orchestral overtures, or suites, the first, in C major,
is perhaps the most witty. Comparisons in respect of absolute
beauty are impertinent. Masterpieces of art should never be compared, except as to technicalities and historical matters. When a
work of art has attained perfection, it is a form of infinity; and with
infinities no process of addition, subtraction, or other arithmetical
operation has the slightest relevance.

The C major Overture is scored for the ordinary string band and
a trio consisting of two oboes and a bassoon. To these resources
we must add the continuo, the harpsichord, or pianoforte in the
hands of a player whose task is to fill in the harmonies from a
figured bass. The string harmony of the C major Suite lies unusually well for euphony without the aid of the continuo; but this
does not mean that a discreet background of keyboard harmony is
not an immense improvement, or rather a restoration of the true
character of Bach's orchestration. The cold and tubby resonance
of Bach's and Handel's string-writing, as left unfilled by the background which these masters deemed essential, is really a modern
invention, and the pious opinion that it represents chastity and
severity is as the hardness of the Greek G or gamma in the Ἐλγιν
marbles.

Where a large string band is used, Bach's trio of oboes and bassoon needs reinforcing. It does not matter what reed instruments
we take for the purpose; clarinets will do just as well as oboes, if
we cannot afford or obtain the overwhelming number of oboes to
which Handel was accustomed. Nobody at the present day knows
exactly what twelve Handelian oboes would sound like, and Handel
himself was more accustomed to twenty. Anyhow, the resemblance to ordinary oboe-tone would be far remoter than the mixture of clarinets and oboes which I propose to use in the tuttis
for purposes of balance. The trio passages, which are especially
marked 'trio' by Bach, should, of course, be played by three
soloists, who may well be given ample time to breathe during the
tuttis.

The title 'overture' applies properly to the first number in this
suite, and means, of course, an overture on Lully's French model,
beginning with a *grave* (in this case rather more flowing and less

jerky than the traditional type) and leading to a lively fugato movement. Here is the theme of the fugue:

Ex. 1.

and the quick movement, which is developed at considerable
length, is very clearly articulated by its natural division between
the tuttis and the trio passages for the three wind instruments. The
grave returns at the end by way of climax.

If this were the overture to an opera, the curtain would rise upon
a ballet. Hence the suite of dances which follows; and hence, con-
versely, the custom of prefacing such suites by a French overture.
The first dance is a French courante, scored for the tutti throughout.

Ex. 2.

I quote the whole first part of this in order to show two points, one
of which does not in this case reach the ear at all unless the continuo player brings it out. Although the time is 3/2, the last note
of the first part is written as if it were 6/4. This is a faint trace of
the fact that the French courante is really in an old kind of triple
time, in which the rhythms of twice three and thrice two are mixed
in a manner which always appears at the cadences and often causes
confusion elsewhere. It is not generally realized that our clear-cut
notions of triple time, such as the rhythm of waltzes and minuets,
are of no great antiquity. Occasional groups of three beats are as
frequent in Palestrina as metrical feet of three syllables in verse;
but not one per cent. of any sixteenth-century master's work is
written ostensibly in triple time, and those in which the triple
time-signature is used are extraordinarily remote from our ideas
of any such rhythm. The other reason why I quote the whole
first strain of this courante is that Bach opens the second strain by
giving the whole of these eight bars a step higher. This is the first
example of a kind of wit peculiarly characteristic of this suite and
of the Flute Suite in B minor.

The next dance is a pair of gavottes, of which the first is scored
for the tutti.

Ex. 3.

The second (alternating) gavotte is scored for the wind trio, but is accompanied by trumpet flourishes on all the violins and violas.

The next dance is a forlane, or forlana, which, I learn from *Grove's Dictionary*, is a favourite lilt with Venetian gondoliers. It is scored for tutti with a running accompaniment of the second violins and violas. The bass supports the harmony with a somewhat derisive approval, until towards the end it is carried away with the other dancers. Perhaps it represents the strokes of the gondolier's pole.

Then there are a pair of minuets, the first scored for tutti—

and the second, a tune of beautiful gravity, scored for the strings in a quiet low position.

Then follows a pair of bourrées. The first is a tutti—

and the second is for the wind trio, and is the only section of the suite in the minor mode.

The suite ends with a pair of passepieds. Of these I quote only the second, because it consists of the whole melody of the first assigned to the violins and violas in unison an octave below its original pitch, with the wind group (not necessarily in solo trio) playing a flowing counterpoint.

Ex. 10.

CCXXIV. LINEAR HARMONY

Bach's works for unaccompanied violin and unaccompanied violoncello triumphantly solve a problem, the very existence of which has escaped the notice of the eminent but misguided composers who have at one time or another added accompaniments to them. When, with most of the rest of Bach's works, these sonatas and suites began to attract attention nearly one hundred years after Bach's death, even such great musicians as Mendelssohn and Schumann failed to dispossess their minds of the idea that no melody longer than the subject of a fugue can support itself without a harmonic accompaniment. Folk-music, which flourishes where harmony is quite undeveloped, had long attracted enthusiastic and respectful attention; and there was no taint of patronage in the zest with which Haydn and Beethoven threw themselves into the task of making large volumes of settings of Scottish, Welsh, and Irish folk-songs at the instigation of the Edinburgh musical publisher Thomson. But even in 1850 it had not yet occurred to anybody that melody could still have aesthetic qualities irrelevant or contradictory to the use of our classical harmonic system as their accompaniment.

There is no evidence that Bach took any interest in folk-music, except in so far as the Lutheran Chorale covers that subject. Composers, like other artists, take a spontaneous interest in anything beautiful that comes naturally into their artistic life; and so long as folk-music remains familiar to their own folk, it will influence them. Otherwise it will have just the same chance of influencing them as any other objects of the enthusiasm of learned societies. The bearing of these unaccompanied string works of Bach upon folk-music is that both rest upon the common ground of cultivating the power of a single thread of unharmonized melody. They cultivate this power in radically different ways. Folk-music, even if it happens to lie along the diatonic major scale, does not attempt to imply a modern or classical harmonic system at all. It is like line-drawing of more or less power and severity which satisfies a decorative and symbolic range of expression without attempting to indicate perspective. You can see from its first seven notes that 'Annie Laurie' is no folk-song; its melody was never conceivable without the support of a pianoforte. Bach's unaccompanied melodies are magnificently powerful line-drawing which shows itself capable of indicating any and every truth of perspective in its draughtsmanship. Of course these works are by no means entirely or mainly without harmony. The violin and the violoncello have four strings, and Bach writes fugues for his unaccompanied violin. Moreover, rapid passages in single notes not only indicate but actually are masses of harmony, if they happen to be arpeggios. Thus the preludes of these suites are masses of harmony as complete as any orchestral harmony on record; and the sarabandes are, for the most part, harmonized in full chords throughout (fuller chords sometimes than the standard violoncello can play, for Bach wrote one suite for a five-stringed instrument, the viola pomposa, said to be his own invention). Still the fact remains that even in the most fully harmonized of these unaccompanied movements there is a constant exercise of the art of making single notes reassert their old prehistoric power of conveying a complete meaning. That is to say, where the melody is unharmonized it is its own bass; hence the miserable failure of even so great a master as Schumann, to say nothing of the really deplorable efforts of Raff, to furnish accompaniments and basses to this music, of which the melody is, like a genuine folk-song, almost invariably the only possible bass. Another topic on which the providers of accompaniments achieve the worst disaster of all is the places in which Bach takes advantage of the possibility that his melody may be ambiguous. Such passages are really impossible to accompany with additional harmonies; not because, like folk-music, they have no harmonic interpretation, but because they are intended to have two or three conflicting meanings, all of them perfectly clear, but leaving it to the event to show how the oracle is infallible. Lastly, it so happens that Bach did transcribe some movements from his solo violin works for fuller combinations. In so doing he did not, as some of the commentators allege, use them as mere sketches, nor did he convey any practical hints to any one who might want to furnish accompaniments to the works. His instrumental art forms are universal. He can turn the violin part of a movement from a concerto into a four-part chorus. He can write an arpeggio prelude for unaccompanied violin and then afterwards turn it into a symphony for organ and orchestra as an introduction to a church cantata: the dimensions and form of the work will remain the same, for the time scale is unalterable, whereas the scale of volume of tone is for Bach a mere accident of material. In order to translate from the solo violin or 'cello to an organ and orchestra we need, not the technical skill to fill out harmonies and interpret ambiguities, but the imagination to conceive the whole work as if it had never existed in the earlier medium. In the history of art there is no greater example of the power of mind over matter.

The suite forms are standardized by Bach in his six violoncello suites and in the English Suites for clavier. There is a great prelude—generally a broadly designed study in scales and arpeggios, but in the C minor suite a full-sized French Overture of which the fugato allegro achieves the paradox of a one-part fugue, distributing its subject over different octaves with antiphonal effect. Then come the dance movements of the suite proper, viz. allemande, courante, sarabande, 'galanterien', and gigue.

The allemande was a rather elaborate and not very dance-like movement in slow common time, but it could, as in the C major Suite, display a sturdy good-natured energy.

The courante is usually of the Italian type, which is in lively triple time, and furnishes a better contrast to the allemande than the French type, with its complicated cross rhythms, used in the English Suites, and in the C minor violoncello suite.

The sarabande is nearly always with Bach the warmest and most lyric part of the suite. After the sarabande come the 'galanterien', the smallest and most tuneful of dances, often in alternating pairs, of which the second member was called trio if and when it is in three-part harmony.

The gigue is, usually, a brilliant finale to the whole. That of the C major Suite has at least two well-contrasted themes, of which the second, with its drumming on open strings, is one of the most picturesque ideas in music before Haydn. Nothing is more remarkable in Bach's suites than the completely individual character of each work and each movement within the extremely precise limits of the form. The six 'cello suites are perhaps in this respect his most remarkable, partly no doubt because of the extraordinary *tour de force* they imply; but the three violin partitas, the four orchestral suites, and the nineteen great clavier suites (the six English and six French suites, the six partitas, and the French Overture) are in no way inferior, except in some cases where the abstruse rhythm of the French courante has set Bach a problem of which there are not many profitable solutions. The task that has in recent years been so triumphantly achieved of securing public recognition of the violoncello suites of Bach in their authentic form, is one of inestimable service to musical culture. It often happens in the history of the appreciation of an art that understanding comes at first through a *tour de force*. Perhaps in this way we may hope that these monumental *tours de force* for violoncello may bring more recognition for the not less beautiful clavier suites.

CCXXV. PRELUDE TO CHURCH CANTATA NO. 29, 'WIR DANKEN DIR, GOTT', FOR ORGAN AND ORCHESTRA

This is the prelude to one of Bach's Rathswahl Cantatas, written for the Sunday service at the time of the municipal elections at Leipzig in 1731.

Violinists and their audiences will at once recognize that we have here in D major a glorification of the prelude to the E major Partita for unaccompanied violin.

There are several modern arrangements of this prelude. The objection to them is not merely the general objection to such things on principle; it is that the arrangers have for the most part shown no knowledge of Bach's own solution of their problem, although the cantata containing it was published by the Bach-Gesellschaft as long ago as 1860. Arrangers who show so little curiosity as to Bach's own methods are not likely to show much grasp of the technical problems of translating 'into the round' a composition originally not only flat but consisting of pure line. It is indeed an extraordinary *tour de force* to find an independent bass for a thing that is already its own bass. Only the fact that most of this prelude consists of arpeggios makes the *tour de force* possible at all. If the movement really were pure line-drawing, like most of these violin solos, its own bass, being also its melody, would not bear doubling, and any other bass would be either stupid or ungrammatical. Even in this prelude there are several places where an arranger can go wrong, and the opportunities have not been neglected. Yet one of my earliest recollections is that of a performance in the 'eighties by Lady Hallé of this prelude in its original key with an orchestral accompaniment of which I distinctly remember the comments of Bach's trumpets, represented delicately by flutes. That is to say, I remember the glorious details of these flutes; and the fact that many years later I recognized them in the trumpets of Bach's score makes me almost certain that Sir Charles Hallé, with characteristic honesty and modesty, produced Bach's own version retransposed to the original key and replacing the organ by the original violin.

Bach's arrangement achieves the miracle of being necessary in every detail though the original was already perfect. In essentials what he has done has been to write a new prelude for orchestra, which combines with the original violin prelude as arranged for the organ, and throws it into high relief by radical contrasts of rhythm. This new orchestral prelude consists mainly of staccato chords distributed antiphonally among the groups of orchestral instruments. Sustained chords now and then strike a deeper and more solemn note, and flourishes of trumpets mark a livelier rhythm, to which the strings add rapid descending scales. Towards the end the livelier rhythm ♩ ♫ ♫♫ | ♩ pervades the whole orchestra, including the drums, and thus becomes a definite theme. Otherwise the form consists merely in the symmetrical balance of long sequences of harmony establishing first the tonic and then the other related keys in a natural order, working round to the tonic again with recognizable repetitions of long sections. One thing only is needed to hold the scheme together, and that is supplied by the perpetual motion of the original prelude, the outlines of which coincide with such details as the occasional descending scales of the strings, while the first two bars (and no others in the whole original prelude) give rise to the livelier rhythmic figure of the orchestra. The efforts of later arrangers are all very much cleverer, and, like a well-known make of safety-match, harmless to those employed in the manufacture.

The cantata 'Wir danken dir, Gott' then proceeds to a chorus which afterwards became (to the same words in Latin) the 'Gratias' of the B minor Mass. But the prelude is an equally appropriate introduction to the mighty double chorus 'Nun ist das Heil', which is published as No. 50 of the Cantatas in the Bach-Gesellschaft edition, but consists of a single chorus, which may or may not be part of a larger work. (See Essay CCIII, vol. 5, p. 71.)

CARL PHILIPP EMANUEL BACH

CCXXVI. SYMPHONY IN D MAJOR

1 *Allego di molto, leading to* 2 *Largo, leading to* 3 *Presto.*

The symphonies of Philipp Emanuel Bach beautifully display the gradual emancipation of the orchestra from its slave-state dependence on the continuo. The emancipation was not the philanthropic process of emancipating slaves. It was the still nobler and more austere problem of teaching the orchestra, including the most aristocratic solo instruments, to serve themselves. To the second volume of *The Heritage of Music* (Oxford University Press) I contributed an essay on Gluck in which I have tried to show that Gluck's reform of opera—that is to say, the whole problem of making music dramatic, instead of merely architectural and decorative—was but one aspect of a radical revolution in the whole art of

music. Social philosophers may consider whether there is not in
political, as well as in artistic, history a negative aspect of such
revolutions that is more evident to contemporaries than the posi-
tive aspect. Certainly, one of the greatest pioneers and emancipa-
tors in the musical revolution of the eighteenth century was loudest
in his complaints that the art of accompanying from a continuo
had declined. His symphonies profess to rely upon a pianoforte,
with chords indicated by a figured bass, to fill up hollow places in
the written score. Philipp Emanuel Bach tells us that this is always
necessary, that the pianoforte is better for the purpose than the
harpsichord (an opinion which I am delighted to find that Dr.
Schweitzer emphatically endorses in the case of John Sebastian's
works), and that, even in open-air performances where you cannot
hear the keyboard instrument at all, its use greatly improves the
general quality of tone. But, if we want an excuse for the neglect
of continuo playing which so alarmed Philipp Emanuel Bach, we
need seek no farther than the remarkable efficiency of his own
orchestration without any such supplement. He is himself obliged
to tell the continuo player to rest for pages together, and the only
passages where he can indicate any figuring at all are simple and
massive outbursts of full harmony. The continuo part is manifestly obsolescent in the very works in which it is most carefully
prescribed.

Nevertheless, I was greatly relieved when I found in an edition
of this symphony older than the current reprints that there was a
genuine continuo instead of the mid-nineteenth century additional
accompaniments which I suspected as being such in the ordinarily
available score. I was also amused to find that my conjectures
were right as to certain places where the Leipzigers of the 'fifties
or 'sixties had found Philipp Emanuel's style not quite literal
enough to be accepted as correct. Their minds had not advanced
from the use of explicit simile to that of metaphor, pure or mixed;
and I found my suspicions well grounded that the symphony has
been carefully amended on the lines of the great Shakespeare
scholar who restored its manifest original common sense to the
sentiment of the Duke who could find (according to the true
reading) 'sermons in books, stones in the running brooks'. Another
thing which the mid-nineteenth century Leipziger abhorred was
abrupt endings, and my head swells with the pride with which
I verified my guess that the end of Philipp Emanuel's finale had
been amended in the style of one of Barry Pain's sententious
domestic tyrants, who observed that 'the inevitable consequences
then happened, as they so often do'.

Philipp Emanuel Bach is, as all the world knows, the link between the polyphonic style and forms of his father and those of

Haydn and Mozart. On this assumption nothing should be easier than to distinguish between those aspects of his art which reflect the past and those which 'coldly predict the style of the future'; and if you happen to quote from an edition of his sonatas by Bülow you can easily find excellent illustrations of both tendencies where-ever Bülow has been pleased to put in something of his own. Even without Bülow's 'splendid emendacity', the history of music is enormously simplified if we do not drag in dates. The trouble begins when we find that Philipp Emanuel Bach was writing in a well-developed style of his own at the time when his father produced the B minor Mass, and that his last set of sonatas was produced in the year of Mozart's *Don Giovanni*. The present symphony was, as far as I can make out, composed in 1780, and is thus a year later than Mozart's epoch-making Paris Symphony. In style and form it has not the remotest resemblance either to his father's work or to the styles of Mozart and Haydn. Unlike the pianoforte works, it is not really on sonata lines at all, except in certain superficial matters. In relation to contemporary music, it is in line with Gluck's overtures, and it shares with them a doubt-ful collateral ancestry with the early concerto grosso. Probably Sammartini's style may be among its origins. At all events, we have the negative evidence that Haydn was very much annoyed with people who saw in his work the influence of Sammartini, who he said was 'a dauber', and who, as I have pointed out in the above-mentioned essay on Gluck, was for that very reason a most useful pioneer in the art of splashing the colours of stage scenery out of a pail.

Philipp Emanuel Bach's Symphony in D has the right of a mature work of art to exist on its own merits. Its historical origins have needed this amount of explanation, because without them the listener is sure to approach the work under preconceptions equally historical in appearance, but entirely misleading as to its character.

Ex. 1.

* Here a disastrous explanatory chord is inserted by the Leipzig editors.

Ex. 2.

The first movement consists of masses of material alternating more or less on concerto grosso lines and connected by an all-pervading rhythmic figure. Of the two groups, one is for strings and the other for wind. They alternate in a scheme not unlike that of Gluck's *Iphigénie en Aulide* (without the introduction), and have, in virtue of a certain amount of recapitulation, the same resemblance to sonata form. The second group contains a definite new theme.

Ex. 3.

At the end of the movement there is a surprising modulation to the dominant of E flat, with a moment of dramatic recitative. Philipp Emanuel Bach's works are often distinguished by some such fantastic event, but his dramatic or recitative-like gestures, while beautiful in themselves, are precisely what deprives the incidents of any importance as an addition to the resources of music. Not many years after this symphony, Haydn put the slow movement of his greatest pianoforte sonata into the key a semitone above that of the first movement; but you will not find Haydn explaining away his paradox by saying 'Then a strange thing happened'. He is not telling fairy tales, but is establishing facts which permanently enlarge the range of music. Far be it from us to say that Philipp Emanuel Bach is mistaken in leaving his harmonic miracle in the state of a fairy-tale surprise. The *Arabian Nights* would not be improved, either as a work of art, or as a study in anthropology, by any explanation of the Magic Carpet as an intelligent anticipation of the aeroplane.

Philipp Emanuel Bach's little miracle leads to a delightful slow tune scored for divided violas and basses doubled by two flutes a couple of octaves higher. Bach explicitly leaves this essentially modern or Haydnesque orchestral effect without help from the continuo. Certainly, nothing better illustrates how inevitable was the doom of that excellent institution. It has, in fact, already attained the state indicated by Barry Pain's hero; the inevitable consequences are beginning to happen often, and the Bread-and-butter-fly has already perished for lack of weak tea with cream in it.

Bach's delicious tune rouses itself to begin a second part, which has the energy to modulate in rising sequences. Such energy is dangerous. The original D major breaks through the unguarded harmonic frontiers, and the symphony ends with a brilliant little jig in binary form.

Some ten or a dozen years after this symphony Haydn produced his ninety-eighth symphony in London and galvanized the gentleman 'at the pianoforte' into life by a brilliant figure near the end of the finale, pencilled into the score, probably during rehearsal. That gentleman ought already to have long been obsolete, but Spohr found him still in possession in London years after Mendelssohn had persuaded the Philharmonic Orchestra to play under the guidance of his baton. Thus slowly did we bid farewell to the continuo generations after we had lost all idea of what it meant.

GLUCK

CCXXVII.   OVERTURE TO 'IPHIGÉNIE EN AULIDE'.
'ORPHEUS AND EURIDICE', ACT II

The symphonies of Philipp Emanuel Bach, rightly understood, show that in reforming—or rather, bringing to dramatic life—the art of opera, Gluck was a pioneer not merely in that matter, but in the whole art of music. In his operas there are two great overtures, that to *Alceste* and that to *Iphigénie en Aulide*. There are also a few great ballets of symphonic dimensions: the chaconne in the Paris version of *Orfeo*, which is expanded from the shorter version in *Iphigénie en Aulide*; and the big dance of Furies in D minor which in *Orfeo* accompanies the change of scene from the banks of Acheron to the scene in the Elysian fields. Gluck's reforms involved no attack upon the insatiable appetite of the French for ballet music. On the contrary, they are the reforms of a musician who was as fond of music as Mozart. In his famous declaration of faith, in the dedication of *Alceste* to the Duke of Tuscany, he declares that his object was to '*reduce* music to its proper function of serving the drama, as well-considered colouring serves the purposes of a well-composed picture'. Mozart, on the contrary, more than once declared that in opera music should be considered first and all the time.

Both Gluck and Mozart are unintelligible as opera writers until we realize that their points of view converge to much the same result. Both of them were supreme masters in the art of bullying their librettists; in fact, greater masters than Wagner, who was sometimes a little shy of bullying himself. It is true that Gluck's first and most important librettist, Calzabigi, flattered himself that he did most of the bullying; but he was a simple soul and Gluck was, among other things, a clever pamphleteer, with a pen almost as venomous as Wagner's. When we come to take the operas of Gluck and of Mozart as they are, we find that with both composers the music comes first and last and all the time, and that what both composers removed was every convention that produced a conflict between musical and dramatic necessity. Gluck and Calzabigi effected their reforms as conscious doctrinaires. Mozart, being unconscious of a duty towards any art but that of music, began as a boy with indulging in fashionable vocal fireworks because he enjoyed them; then in his first really great opera, *Idomeneo* (which is powerfully and obviously influenced by Gluck's *Alceste*), he began to feel, as we feel, that the cadenzas and formulas were intrusive; and he ended, in *Cosi fan tutte* and *Die Zauberflöte*, by rationalizing them and satirizing them where he did not abolish them altogether. In the meantime he bullied his librettists and kept them in a perpetual state of exasperated astonishment at the way in which he took their modest schemes out of their hands and turned their puppets into demigods. Calzabigi claimed that he furnished Gluck with precise directions as to the rise and fall, as well as the rhythms, required for the singing of his verses. Perhaps he did; in which case Gluck deserves the highest praise for his tact in suffering a fool gladly for the sake of that fool's grains of common sense. We need not suppose that he followed the directions.

As for Gluck's own modest avowal that he *reduced* music to its proper function of colouring the drama fitly, the plain truth is that Calzabigi enabled Gluck's music to reign as supremely as Mozart's by the contrary process of reducing the action to something considerably less than that of a ballet. He had published an edition of Metastasio's works which that poet regarded with special favour; and Metastasio is not to blame for the fact that his scheme of opera was so fool-proof and gave such universal satisfaction to full-sized theatre troupes that not only Handel and Hasse but every contemporary, down to the worst, composed his operas without the slightest exercise of the brain. The Metastasio scheme was excellent common sense. For the conflict between music and action is the conflict between poetry and action. Even the Elizabethan audience, no less than the Elizabethan poet, wished the action to be shown in dialogue of business-like efficiency culminating at every possible point of repose in a tableau during which poetry might display itself. Poetry and action could attain a high temperature simultaneously whenever there was any dramatic tension in the mere awaiting of a doubtful event. The only trouble with Metastasio was that he was a born *improvisatore* with a fatal facility in ornamentation, and so serviceable a mastery in constructing plots that every one of his operas could provide work for a troupe of seven actors, and keep the poet himself too busy ever to concentrate his poetry on a focus of genuine passion.

It was all this pleasant work which Calzabigi swept away. For two of the three acts of *Orfeo* there is only one actor, Orpheus himself. In the Elysian fields Euridice may be replaced with great advantage to the drama by an unnamed chorus-leader. In the third act she has the tragically important part of exasperating Orpheus into looking upon her face before he has brought her into the light of mortal day. Calzabigi is obviously in great difficulty as to how to execute this part of the story at all. We know that Orpheus has been told by Eros, or Amor (who in the first act has a small part as the messenger of the gods), that the condition on which he can fetch Euridice from the world of shades is that he must not look upon her face until he has brought her into daylight. But Amor has not told him that he must not explain this to her; and it is clear that, if Orpheus did explain it, not even such a goose as Calzabigi's Euridice would have plagued him into breaking the condition. The miracle of Calzabigi's libretto, and of Gluck's setting of it, is that it nevertheless does result in what is not only the first, but remains to this day one of the most intense, of all mature music dramas. It is not surprising that the story should from the outset have fascinated musicians. The very first opera was Peri's *Euridice* (1600). It made an immense impression, eclipsed seven years later by Monteverdi's *Orfeo*. I have not space here to recapitulate what I have written in an essay on Gluck contributed to *The Heritage of Music*. The history and importance of Gluck's operatic reforms are far more complicated than they appear to be from the accounts of orthodox historians. What remains for me to do in this analysis is to explain why I preface Act II of *Orfeo* by the Overture to *Iphigénie en Aulide*; and then to give a short account of all the music in question.

In the famous Preface to *Alceste* Gluck says that the overture ought to give some indication of what is to follow, and, in fact, to be a kind of argument of the play. He had not formulated this doctrine when he wrote *Orfeo*, and in any case he had no

Wagnerian *leitmotiv* system by which his overture could definitely foreshadow musical themes used in the opera. Moreover, even his ripest works lived, like Handel's, if not more so, by taking in each other's washing; and the last of his great operas, *Armide*, uses the Overture to a probably quite unrevivable work called *Telemacco*. I do not remember whether the Overture to *Orfeo* has had any previous use; what is quite clear is that its sole function is to throw into relief the funeral rites of which most of the first act consists. Pious commentators quote this or that more or less dignified formula from it as representing Orpheus's descent into Hades, or as typifying his heroic resolve; but they might as well quote any chance passage from the symphonies of Philipp Emanuel Bach. The Overture to *Iphigénie en Aulide* has, indeed, a direct connexion with its drama; and, in fact, its last phrase is ended by the rise of the curtain upon the entry of the heart-broken Agamemnon, who sings its introductory theme:

Ex. 1.

Dia - - - ne im - pi - toy - a - ble.

But we need not scruple to use this heroic overture as a prelude to the second act of *Orfeo*. One hero in dire distress is as good as another, if his problem be worthy for the gods to solve. The Overture to *Iphigénie en Aulide* shows all the finest features of Gluck's orchestration, which, by the way, are treated with the utmost reverence by Wagner in his version, which we adopt for concert use.

Many misunderstandings as to tempo have resulted in performances which sound like a schoolboy's literal construe of Euripides; in particular the confusion between the French *grave* and the Italian *grave*.

Ex. 2.
Grave.

There is no evidence that this mighty theme is more than a little slower than the semiquaver tutti which follows it, and which would be intolerable if spelt out slowly.

A second group brings gentle pathetic elements into the scheme; and the treatment of the horn and oboe, while avoiding direct anticipation, decidedly resembles one of the most epoch-making passages in all music, Agamemnon's lines beginning 'J'entends retentir dans mon sein le cri plaintif de la nature'.

Ex. 3.

Wagner most ingeniously and reverently ends the overture for concert performance by resuming the introduction (Ex. 1) exactly as Agamemnon takes it up on the rise of the curtain. Not for worlds would I part with the slight imperfection of Wagner's end, which presents with priceless subtlety the evidence that Wagner cannot, with all his reverence, accommodate himself to the classical time-scale. Every naïve listener, and all the non-Wagnerians of past generations, have felt that this end is at least four bars too long. But if you try to reduce it, you will find that the problem is insoluble, which may be said of every adaptation of one composer's work by another, and of most efforts of a composer to adapt his own work.

At all events, there is nothing in the Overture to *Iphigénie en Aulide* which prevents it from being an admirable concert-room introduction to the second act of *Orfeo*. Wagner's end can be followed with excellent effect by the awe-inspiring sounds upon which the curtain rises on the banks of Acheron. According to the rather vague stage directions, the Furies and other shades are moving in some kind of dance, though the music is exceedingly slow, when the sound of Orpheus's lyre alarms them. The Furies give out the first five lines of their chorus, asking who this audacious mortal can be. Except for the places where they interrupt Orpheus with cries of *No*, their rhythm is exactly that of 'God save the King', and in the style of their melody, their harmony, and their monotone, Gluck has achieved an astonishing majesty and consistency. Their highest indignation is expressed by singing in octaves or unison. One of the most wonderful features is the representation of Cerberus. A more dangerous occasion for bathos could hardly be conceived, but I will venture to assert that nobody has ever dreamt of thinking the threats of Gluck's Cerberus grotesque.

I prefer to leave without quotation the series of passages in which the pleadings of Orpheus alternate with the lessening opposition of the Furies. One incident must be illustrated from the passage which the Furies interrupt with cries of *No*. In the first fine careless rapture of Rameau's discovery of the fundamental bass, Rousseau poured out pages of enthusiastic theoretic nonsense about the enharmonic conflict between B natural and C flat as the Furies become more menacing; which nonsense Berlioz afterwards annihilated in his best and most derisive vein, while far transcending Rousseau's highest efforts in deifying Gluck.

Ex. 4.

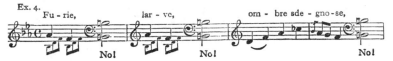

But I have not met with a commentator who has noticed what seems to me the crucial point in the conflict between Orpheus and the Furies, and which is the more remarkable because a similar point happens in the Andante of Beethoven's G major Concerto, a movement which Liszt compared not inaptly to Orpheus taming wild beasts. At the last *No*, the Furies, who have been menacing Orpheus with an ominous rise of pitch at each step of his melody, melt into harmony.

Ex. 5.

Further musical illustrations do not seem necessary. Berlioz, in his generous jealousy for Gluck, protested indignantly at the use of trombones elsewhere than to support the *No* of the Furies. It is true that the trombones do not appear in Gluck's autograph, but there is cogent evidence that the extant trombone parts were used under Gluck's direction; and the fact is that a more shocking mess than a Gluck autograph, even if it begins like a fair copy, is hardly to be found in the history of paleography.

The long ballet that covers the change of scene to the Elysian fields is one of Gluck's finest instrumental movements, and can be followed without the aid of quotations. So also can the exquisite Elysian ballets upon which the curtain rises again. The flute solo which serves as a kind of trio to the first *air de ballet* gives that Undine of instruments such a soul as only Bach had hitherto granted to it. But perhaps the climax of all Gluck's inspirations is the first Elysian chorus, the tune of which is according to some directions assigned to Euridice—and no wonder, as the actress of that thankless part has otherwise nothing to sing until the third act. There are many greater composers than Gluck, but if, like Matthew Arnold, we wish to keep in our memories certain unsurpassable lines as 'touchstones for poetry' or for melody, I do not know any touchstone more capable of eclipsing lesser melodies than the tune of the first Elysian chorus.

Ex. 6.

C

Its emotional effect is quite extraordinary; and one of the most experienced conductors of opera whom I know frankly confesses that a performance of Gluck's *Orfeo* is, in spite of an apparatus which is primitive in every technical and dramatic direction, more exhausting to him from the concentration of its emotional power than a whole cycle of Wagner's *Ring*.

The Happy Shades disperse, and Orpheus enters upon the scene alone. The wonderful arioso during which he gazes around might well deserve another quotation, but defies reduction to much less than the full score, which is remarkably elaborate as judged by the standards of any period. In the original Italian version it was still more elaborate, and there is no doubt that the Parisian version has eliminated unnecessary and disturbing features of the scoring.

The history of the Paris version of *Orfeo* is very sad, and its consequences threaten to be sadder still. Every piece of music that Gluck added for Paris, and every alteration in the essential musical rhetoric, was an incalculable improvement. But it was all vitiated by the fact that the part of Orpheus was transposed from contralto to tenor. This involved dislocating the whole key-system of the scene with the Furies; and the dislocation is one of the most ghastly pieces of mangling that could be conceived. How the eminent scholars who brought out the great Pelletan-Damcke *édition de luxe* of Gluck's chief works could bring themselves to put this forward as the definitive form of *Orfée et Euridice* is one of the mysteries which only patriotism—or, rather, nationalism at its worst—can explain. Many people see the obvious objections to representing Orpheus by a woman. Gluck's Orpheus was never represented by a woman. The great but unfortunate artists who sung him with a contralto voice represent a disgrace to civilization which only the most hateful of racial prejudices could have the criminal audacity to revive. Those who can remember the performances of *Orfeo* by the sisters Ravogli in the early 'nineties will reject with indignant contempt the idea that there was anything half so unnatural to Gluck's music, or to nature itself, in such a performance as the ruining of the whole composition which he had the weakness to accept while adapting, and in many respects improving, his work for Paris. The version performed in London somewhere about 1890 by the sisters Ravogli was ideally in the spirit of Gluck in every respect that I can recall, except in the fact that the bravura aria with which Gluck ends the first act in defiance of all his own propaganda, was retained. I cannot verify the date of this wonderful performance, though I can remember most of the details and can certify that the version was as it stands in my own excellent Peters full score, which was given to me in February

1890. The sisters Ravogli were duly commemorated in early editions of *Grove's Dictionary*. My up-to-date one has removed them to make room for names (not necessarily in the same part of the alphabet) which I might not feel inclined to consider equally worthy. The current English version seems to me to deal as well as can be expected with the tangle of compromises that have been forced on Gluck by translation from Calzabigi's Italian into I forget whose French, and re-translation from the French back into something which has to differ from Calzabigi where Gluck has altered the music. Nobody should blame our singers for the common consensus of Gluck's music and four modern languages to pronounce the name of Euridice as wrongly as we pronounce Trafalgar. But piety towards the French text seems to me rather superfluous. We have our own provincial standard of poetic diction, and this disqualifies us from appreciating the Greek simplicity of Racine; but I do not think that the French translator, writing under Gluck's own eye, achieved Racine's plainness when he made the Elysian spirits promise that Euridice was to return *avec de nouveaux attraits!* Racine literally translated may seem to us to fall into flat prose, but I should be surprised to learn that he was capable of so misinterpreting the condition in which Orpheus would prefer to rejoin Euridice. Calzabigi was no such fool. What he said was *Euridice già riprende la primiera sua beltà.*

The latest, and almost the most infuriating, stage in the history of *Orfeo* is that editions are now being published of the pure Italian text minus all the substantial improvements with which Gluck made the chief roles worthy of the genius of the sisters Ravogli. Before long it will become difficult to get an edition of *Orfeo* that combines the essentials of Gluck's final thoughts with the integrity of his original plans. I have no use for a purism and a scholarship which refuses to make the compromises necessary for such an end.

MOZART

CCXXVIII. SYMPHONY IN D MAJOR (PARIS SYMPHONY).
(KÖCHEL'S CATALOGUE, NO. 297)
1 *Allegro assai.* 2 *Andantino.* 3 *Allegro.*

Mozart's Paris Symphony is famous as a work of great historical importance. While I am writing this analysis an eminent colleague is stimulating the musical intelligentsia of Harvard by inveighing against reverence for the classics; which in some forms does, indeed, as he says, clutter up the minds of people whose opinions might otherwise become independent and valuable. An apparent reverence for the classics is as likely as any other form of snobbishness to mask an inactive mind which is too vacant to be charged with being cluttered up with anything at all. Accordingly, it cannot be said to do any harm so far as it goes, since it goes nowhere. But I know nothing that can clutter up the mind more ruinously than a preoccupation with the squalid conditions to which all artists, great and small, accommodated themselves with more or less difficulty or complacence in periods that have become classical. Some ingenuity may be wasted in imputing psychological thought to Shakespeare when he is producing inconsistencies which are more completely explained as crass accommodation to inartistic conditions, or even as carelessness. The more we know of such things the better, so long as we realize that a man of genius cannot suppress his real self, however much he may try; unless, indeed, he stops working altogether. Under mundane conditions, art may attain three heavens: one, the highest, which is above all conflicts; the second, where an artist enjoys accommodating himself to his world and is above consciousness of his irony; and the lowest, but still a heaven, in which he writes with his tongue in his cheek. Below this lies hell, into which Mozart did not descend even in his church music. Of purgatory I have no official information. We Protestants have our limitations.

Mozart's trials in Paris may have brought him down to the third heaven, but I see no evidence that he did not enjoy the concessions to Parisian taste which make the features of the Paris Symphony almost amount to a code of etiquette. He took such advantage of these concessions that he enlarged the Parisians' ideas of music almost as extensively and quite as deeply as Gluck had enlarged their ideas of music drama. He writes to his father on 11 September 1778, that his earlier symphonies wouldn't do there: 'Our taste in Germany is for length, but really it is better to be short and sweet.' This was apropos of the advice that the Parisians preferred symphonies to have no 'repeats'; and, accordingly, the Paris Symphony is the first important sonata-work before Beethoven in which there are no long repeats. Yet it is longer than any of Mozart's earlier symphonies. For Parisian audiences needed repetitions of phrases on the spot as much as the audiences of any mob orator. To this day French composers tend, like Couperin and brilliant and colourful Russians like Rimsky-Korsakov, to say each sentence twice over: sometimes in other words, like the parallelism of Hebrew poetry, but more often in the same words.

Another instruction which amused Mozart very much was that every symphony should begin with a *grand coup d'archet*. Mozart obeyed instructions, and, before the symphony was played, was well satisfied that it would please the few French people whose opinion was worth anything. As for stupid people, he saw no great misfortune if it didn't please them; but he had hopes that even donkeys would find something to like in it, and above all, he had not muffed the *premier coup d'archet*. He didn't see why the dolts made such a ridiculous fuss about an orchestra that just begins all together as in other places. A friend told him that an excellent musician, Dal Abaco, was asked whether he had been at Paris and heard a *Concert Spirituel*, and what did he think about the *premier coup d'archet?* 'Did you hear it?' 'Yes,' said Dal Abaco, 'I heard the first stroke and the last; and the last pleased me better.' Well, here is what Mozart made of the *premier coup d'archet* and of the need of mob-orator repetition—

As for the mob-orator repetition, it was as much a need to the twenty-year old Mozart at this stage of his development as it was to any contemporary audience. But you will notice: first, that the *coup d'archet* has found its organic and thematic answer in the rhythm of the wind instruments, whose every note is so significant that the second flute is an individual who prepares for the entry of the first flute. Moreover, the repetition expands. Mozart, at the age of twenty, cannot make a concession to the stupidest Parisian conventions without producing musical forms decidedly more advanced than anything you can find in the phrasing of Schumann's Quintet, with all its wealth of epigram; and so it is through the whole symphony. There is not a note without its permanent value, and Mozart is able to use the stupid Parisian conventions as a means of educating the Parisians out of them. He was instructed that finales ought also to begin with a *coup d'archet* in unison, instead of which he began his finale with eight bars piano for the violins alone. As he expected, he heard an excited 'Hush, hush' from the audience at the beginning. Then came the forte, and at the same moment a burst of applause; whereupon Mozart, who had been in deadly anxiety at the horrors of the rehearsal, went with feelings of great relief to the Palais Royal and ate an excellent ice.

I need not quote many of the twenty or thirty other themes with which the symphony is comfortably packed.

As far as I can see, Ex. 2 must be the theme of which Mozart writes: 'In the middle of the first allegro was a passage which I knew could not fail to please. All the audience were charmed by it, and there was great applause, but as I knew when I wrote it what an effect it would make, I brought it round an extra time at the end of the movement, with the same result, and so got my applause da capo.'

Monsieur Le Gros, the director of the *Concerts Spirituels*, declared that this was the best symphony he had ever heard, which, as
Parry remarks, is not be to wondered at, considering that nothing
like it had ever been written before; but he did not like the andante,
and told Mozart that it modulated too much and was too long.
'This impression', said Mozart ,'arose merely because the audience
had forgotten to clap so noisily and so persistently as in the first
movement and finale. The andante pleased me and all connoisseurs
and amateurs, and most of the audience, best of all. It's the exact
opposite of what Le Gros says. It's quite natural—and short; but
in order to please him and, as he believes, many others, I have
made another andante. Each is right in its way, because each has
its own character, but I like the second still better.' The second
andante is, accordingly, the one that survives in the Paris Symphony. Mozart took unusual pains over the second andante, revising
it so much that he had to clear it up by writing an extra fair copy.
Le Gros and his like cannot have had the slightest conception of
the meaning of Mozart's alterations; but they were doubtless
flattered by the fact that he had written a new movement to please
them. Here is its main theme—

Ex. 3.

and here is the beginning of the finale which surprised the Parisians
out of their dependence on the *premier coup d'archet*—

Ex. 4.

Grateful as the Reid Orchestra is for all evidences of public recognition, we are glad that the music-lovers of Edinburgh are not so
immediate in the expression of their opinions as the public of the
Concerts Spirituels in 1778.

Mozart was afraid of no one; and he took the opportunity of beginning his second group with a fugato which must have impressed the Parisians as very learned. For the orchestra it has a characteristic advantage: like the rhythmic figure of the initial *coup d'archet* (Ex. 1), it gives opportunity for every member of the wind band to assert himself as an individual, the second player answering or anticipating the first.

Ex. 5.

However much the historian's mind may be cluttered up by his knowledge of the philistinisms with which Mozart dealt so diplomatically in the Paris of 1778, there is no denying that, while these philistinisms may have prevented Mozart at the age of twenty-two from offering the Parisians work that might anticipate the depth of his later thoughts, he thoroughly enjoyed enlarging—or, rather, revolutionizing—their notions of craftsmanship by introducing to them all, and rather more than all, the refinements of orchestral technique developed at Mannheim, such as the crescendo, the diminuendo, and other *coups d'archet* than the first and last.

MOZART

CCXXIX. ARIA, FROM 'DIE ENTFÜHRUNG', 'MARTERN ALLER ARTEN'

Mozart and Gluck are the two great reformers of opera, and the way in which Mozart reformed it is a most disconcerting lesson for Earnest Persons. He reformed it because, though, as all Italians averred throughout most of the nineteenth century, his genius was melancholy, he was an inveterate comedian and sinfully fond of music. The first opera which brought about the reform was *Die Entführung aus dem Serail*. The librettist of that work meant to produce a harmless *Singspiel* with some Turkish local colour, but Mozart ran away with both ends of the project. The exploit of the young Englishman who rescued his wife from the Turk's harem had its heroic side, and the poor librettist, Bretzner, found to his disgust that Mozart insisted on imposing the noblest sentiments upon Belmont and Constanze. On the other hand, Mozart had a shocking facility of his own in rhymes for patter-singing, the Rabelaisian tendencies of which he could, under dire necessity, keep within bounds producible before a public less squeamish than ours. Hence, the part of Osmin, the keeper of the Turk's harem, also became a thing mainly of Mozart's creation.

The tremendous emotional concentration of Gluck's music disguises from us what is self-evident in what we must call Calzabigi's plots, that his reform of opera was ascetic to the verge of annihilation. Mozart's serious opera, *Idomeneo*, is influenced by Gluck's sublimity and emotional power in immediate juxtaposition to luxuries which exaggerate much of what Gluck sternly rejected. This, again, is disguised by the fact that Mozart is an immeasurably greater musician than any previous opera writer, so that it is difficult to say that his most reactionary procedures have not some element of progress in them. In *Die Entführung*, where the dialogue is spoken and the mixture of serious heroics and farcical comedy is extreme, we find ourselves able to acquiesce in anything Mozart is kind enough to give us. His music is so inveterately dramatic that it was bound to reform the music drama, even if it flew in the face of every principle that Gluck held sacred. Any attempt to rationalize the *mise en scène* of Constanze's great aria, 'Martern aller Arten', is doomed to failure. Mozart is seized with a violent combined attack of character-portrayal and music. The result is a quadruple concerto for flute, oboe, violin, and violoncello which serves as background and framework to a heroic coloratura aria displaying the character of Constanze, the noble English wife imprisoned in the house of a not less noble Turk and defying him when he threatens to insist upon his rights of conquest. Away with all minor problems of what the poor man is to do with his hands or his gestures while the heroic woman presumably walks round the room or poses as a statue until the ritornello of the quadruple concerto is over! Probably the best thing is to pose the whole group as a waxwork and listen to the music. Immense as this aria is, and often as it is cut even in concert performances, the autograph shows that Mozart had already cut from it one passage of 12 bars and another of 15. His own account when he later apologized for the aria was that he simply could not stop when he was writing it; and why should he? There are times when a dramatic situation is static enough for good music to be more important. The present situation is that the excellent Bassa Selim, who turns out in the end to be a perfect gentleman, is pointing out to Constanze that she is absolutely in his power, that his patience is not illimitable, that he is within his rights, and that torments of all kinds await those who disobey him. To which she replies in a noble tirade—but not just yet. The six themes of the quadruple concerto must be exposed and concluded after a cadenza before Constanze can begin. Here are the six themes, which I designate by the sentiments which they 'register':

Ex. 1.

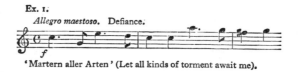

'Martern aller Arten' (Let all kinds of torment await me).

Ex. 2. Conciliation.

Ex. 3.

'Des Himmels Segen belohne dich' (Heaven's blessing reward you for mercy).

Ex. 4. More defiance.

Ex. 5. Pleading.

Ex. 6. The Last Word (Whose?).

Not only does Constanze work these six themes, cadenza and all, into concerto form, but, finding Bassa Selim unresponsive, she interpolates an independent movement in double quick time, demanding (in vain) that he should lose his temper, and triumphing in the hope of final release by death. This substitute for a development-section makes the recapitulation of the concerto stand out in beautiful relief, and furnishes a noble work with a grand close on 'der . . . Tod!'

CCXXX. ARIA FROM 'LA CLEMENZA DI TITO'

The corno di bassetto, a favourite instrument of Mozart's, is difficult to procure nowadays; and the ordinary alto clarinet of modern commerce has, with the sublime contemptuousness of Big Business, neglected to supply it with the bottom notes required by Mozart, who wrote the only music worth playing upon it. For this reason the only one of the great arias in *La Clemenza di Tito* that is heard in the concert-room is the weakest: the big aria by Sesto, 'Deh per questo istante solo'. Another aria in the role of Sesto, 'Parto, ma tu ben mio', has a clarinet obbligato, which, in relation to its pitch, needs the same extra keys as the corno di bassetto in passages difficult to arrange without mutilation. The history of this special instrument is unknown. There is an unfinished clarinet quintet, the sketch of which breaks off soon after Mozart has betrayed a manifest absence of mind as to the downward compass of the instrument. The plan of this work, as revealed by its opening, became gloriously realized in the Clarinet Quintet which we possess.

There cannot have been any oversight about the clarinet part in Sesto's aria 'Parto', because *La Clemenza di Tito* was written for and performed at the wedding of the Emperor of Austria to an Italian princess, who graciously remarked that the work was *una porcheria tedesca*. Mozart had, indeed, patched his German piggery as quickly as possible in the intervals of composing and producing *Die Zauberflöte*, and at inns where the coach stopped to bait in journeys between Vienna and Prague. Neither the libretto, which is Metastasio at his stiffest and stuffiest, nor the occasion was inspiring; and, except for a few bright spots, such as the overture and the aria 'Non più di fiori', the score of *Clemenza di Tito* as a whole gives one a nightmare impression of the *Zauberflöte* having dried up and gone wrong. Among the bright spots I insist upon including a passage from the first finale which Professor Dent quotes in his standard work on Mozart's operas with averted eye, as anticipating the style of Dykes, the author of our treacliest Victorian church music. I respectfully submit that, on the contrary, the end of the first act of *Tito* is theatre music of the highest quality; and that Mozart is not to blame if the appropriate lugubrious chords of the chorus behind the stage inspired the Reverend John Bacchus Dykes to reproduce it in church before the altar. I have my own weakness for treacle in season.

The greatest thing in *Tito* is, unquestionably, Vitellia's aria, 'Non più di fiori'. In comparison, the better-known aria, 'Deh per questo istante solo', is not only a pale substitute, but almost a caricature. Just compare with Vitellia's noble second theme (Ex. 3) the tune, almost identical in rhythm, to which Sesto asks: 'Can a heart endure such suffering and not die of grief?'

Ex. 1.

Tan - to affan-no sof - fre un co - re, ne si mo - re di do - lor?

Obviously it can, with a tune like that! Of course, Sesto must punctuate his singing with sobs, and the repeated chords must be played appropriately, and not so as to suggest the syllables 'tum-tum'; but it would be difficult to find a more extreme illustration of the efficient perfunctory elasticity of classical convention. But in 'Non più di fiori' Mozart rises to the occasion as if stung, like Vitellia herself, by the words of Servilia, the singer of a small part, who has just told Vitellia in a graceful minuet: 'If you can't do better for him than tears, all your weeping won't help. This useless pity which you feel seems to me mighty like cruelty.' Exit Servilia, while the orchestra finishes her minuet with a couple of exquisite curtsies. Vitellia is now alone with her thoughts. During the first act of the opera she has been keeping her lover Sesto at a distance, until he has executed his promise to her that he will assassinate the Emperor. As soon as she has sent Sesto about his business, she learns that the Emperor has dismissed her rival Berenice, and has sent for her to make her his Empress. She cannot recall Sesto, and the Capitol is fired to the strains which inspire Dykes.

The second act is concerned with the Emperor's clemency; and Vitellia's great aria occupies the penultimate scene. In recitative she meditates as follows:

Now is the moment, O Vitellia, to test thy firmness. Hast thou the courage to see thy faithful Sextus lifeless?

Sextus, who loves thee more than his life, who became a criminal only through thy fault, who obeyed and adored thee through all thy cruelty and injustice, who has been so faithful to thee in the presence of death? And would'st thou now, well knowing what thou dost, calmly go to the bride-chamber of Augustus? Alas, I shall see Sextus before my eyes. I shall fear lest the very stones and winds betray my secret to Titus. (*With resolution*) I will fall at his feet and reveal everything. My crime shall at least diminish the crime of Sextus, if it cannot excuse it. Farewell, all hopes of empire and espousals.

Ex. 2.   RONDO
Larghetto.

No more shall Hymen come down to weave beautiful chains of flowers. I see Death approaching me through myriad cruel torments.

(*Allegro*) Me miserable, what am I? Surely they who behold my sorrow would have mercy upon me.

Ex. 3.

Chi ve - des - se il mio do - lo - re, pur a - vria di me pie - tà.

In the coda of the aria, this last noble theme is matched by an equally distinguished passage, where the voice and the corno di bassetto sing together in double counterpoint.

Ex. 4.
Corno di bassetto.

Voice.

with Flute 8*va*.

with Violin

Students of instrumentation should note that the corno di bassetto makes an admirable bass to the voice, but that when the parts are reversed, so that the voice becomes bass, the violins must support it; and that, moreover, the violins will make a bass to the corno di bassetto even when they go above it at the notes marked with an asterisk.

MOZART

CCXXXI.   OVERTURE TO 'COSÌ FAN TUTTE'

Not only the wit of Da Ponte, but the irony of Mozart's music in *Così fan tutte* baffled their contemporaries and the literal-minded romanticists of the nineteenth century. In my young days the orthodox view of *Così fan tutte* was that it showed a reactionary falling-off into operatic conventionality after the epoch-making advances that Mozart had achieved in *Figaro* and *Don Giovanni*. We had to wait for Richard Strauss to point out to us early in the present century that *Così fan tutte* is a masterpiece of parody and irony. The story is ridiculously improbable, and the improbability becomes infuriating if, as has been averred, it was founded on fact. The cynical old bachelor has persuaded the two heroes to test the fidelity of the two heroines by pretending to go off to the wars, and returning, fantastically disguised, in order to make love to each other's lady. After violent protestations and sham suicides, the disguised lovers are accepted; but the wedding-breakfast is interrupted by their sudden return as themselves. On such altitudes of farce emotions are extremely lofty, but their boiling-point is low, and the wedding-breakfast is quickly redistributed in the right way. The first requirement of the highest order of parody is that it should take its opportunity of being obviously more beautiful than the things parodied. The things parodied are severely limited by irrelevant realities. As Stevenson's young poet of the Cream Tarts discovered, when 'opulent orotunda' is obviously what you want to say, some nonsense about sense interferes. From any such nonsense *Così fan tutte* is free, and takes its opportunity to become a miracle of irresponsible beauty unlike anything else in Mozart. No other opera has such a wealth of ensemble-music, and such a variety of forms. All the emotions are, *ex hypothesi*, either superficial or feigned. Mr. Christie, the Maecenas of Glyndebourne, has hit the mark in describing *Così fan tutte* as a dream.

The Overture is one of the funniest things Mozart ever wrote. Its themes, alternating their whisperings and chatterings with a hilarious kind of Hallelujah Chorus, tell us in Mozart's language that the persons of this dream are, humanly speaking, rubbish, but far too harmless for any limbo less charitable than the eternal laughter of Mozart. The only theme I need quote is the solemn motto of the introduction and of the whole opera: 'That's what all girls do.'

Co - sì fan tut - te! Co - sì fan

Presto.

tut - - - - te! &c.

BEETHOVEN

CCXXXII. FIFTEEN VARIATIONS AND FUGUE, 'PROMETHEUS', OP. 35

Although in analysing the finale of Beethoven's Eroica Symphony I go so far as to deprecate thinking of the remarkable set of variations on the same material written by Beethoven a few years earlier, I believe that that finale cannot fail to gain in impressiveness if the earlier work has been duly appreciated during the same concert.

The Variations (Op. 35) are a very complete and perfect work, eminently characteristic of the pianoforte and marking an epoch in the history of the variation form. The finale of the Eroica is the finale of a symphony, and, while it contains the principal ideas of these earlier Variations and Fugue transformed into an orchestral style unusually rich and free even for Beethoven, it leaves an immense amount unsaid for which the Pianoforte Variations have abundant scope. The Variations are in the position of the epic poem with its almost unlimited room for description and rhetoric. The finale of the symphony has all the heightened and direct effect of drama, with all its stern practical and aesthetic necessity for compression and immediate action. The difference between the two works is thus no mere question of Beethoven's progress in musical thought. For instance, it is right for the symphonic finale to begin abruptly with an outburst in a foreign key; but it is right for the Pianoforte Variations as an independent work to begin simply with an introductory tonic chord, which, by the way, is in the same position as the first chords of the whole Eroica Symphony.

Then Beethoven proceeds to build up his work as in the symphonic finale, with the grotesque bare bass of his theme. Speaking strictly from the point of view of the work in itself, this absurd bass is the real theme, and Beethoven might perhaps have called it so if the fully harmonized tune had not existed years before in the Prometheus Ballet. On the other hand, much of the point of this bare bass lies in its extreme grotesqueness, which in the second part amounts to a sheer practical joke; and even the counterpoints with which it is gradually clothed in the three sections marked à 2, à 3, à 4 (i.e. duet, trio, and quartet) are all of the nature of formulas; so that there is no doubt that when the tune sails in on the top with a dance-rhythm accompaniment it is what we have been waiting for all the time. You will find this Tune (which I spell with a capital T) with its bass in Ex. 6 of my analysis of the Eroica Symphony.

Now we come to the variations officially recognized as such.

Var. I ornaments the Tune with brilliant arabesques.

Var. II retains much of the outline of the Tune in still more brilliant passage-writing.

Var. III. In Variation III only the harmonic scheme is preserved, and the bold pianoforte writing remarkably anticipates the key-board technique of a later generation of pianists with whose tendencies Beethoven was by no means wholly in sympathy. On the strength of this Variation a very plausible case might be made for Beethoven's claim to have invented some of the features of the virtuoso technique of Thalberg and even of Henselt.

Var. IV is a running étude for the left hand, very quiet.

Var. V is a graceful cantabile in the lightest open part-writing, with much of the melody in the bass as well as on the surface.

Var. VI. In Variation VI the Bass is abandoned and the Tune is ingeniously put into C minor by mere alteration of the harmonies without transposition. Just in the last two bars the harmony is screwed back again into the tonic so as to lead to

Var. VII, which is mostly in two-part canon in the octave. Like all Beethoven's canons, this is a humorously crude performance; but let no one be misled by some otherwise excellent authorities to suppose that it expresses nothing but an inability to handle the technique of such forms. It expresses the spirit of caricature in which an archaic form may most effectively enter into a work which is eminently brilliant and full of allusive wit. For this very reason there is now a call for a deeper note; and

Var. VIII begins quietly with one of the great romantic moments in this work.

Var. IX reacts from this in very brilliant and sonorous pianoforte style which can only fill one with astonishment that contemporaries should have thought even Weber, to say nothing of Hummel, Beethoven's equal in the treatment of the instrument.

Var. X is brilliant in another way, entirely pianissimo until the second part, where a harmonic stroke of genius lifts the whole conception to a higher intellectual plane, or rather shows the real nature of Beethoven's interest in brilliant technique. Throughout these variations, as also in the Eroica finale, you may expect the beginning of the second part of the theme to be the place in which strange things may happen; and what happens here is that the pitch is suddenly screwed up from B flat to C flat.

Var. XI is graceful and playful with an entirely new melody (by the way, the original Tune has hardly been recognizable since Var. VI, except in very faint outline in Var. X; while the Bass has long refrained from obtruding itself at all). The second part of this 11th Variation again contains a beautiful harmonic feature, though not one which radically changes the key.

Var. XII is another interesting pianoforte étude in humorous dialogue between the right hand and the left; while Var. XIII brings the bravura aspect of the work to a very original climax with a device extremely troublesome to the player (so that, like almost all Beethoven's brilliancies, it has never been imitated since) but hilariously effective.

The natural reaction from this is the sad sobriety of Var. XIV, in the minor mode. The long-lost Bass does duty as a tune with a new melody below it. In the repetitions the Bass resumes its proper position below, and another new melody is given above. When this variation has reached its despondent end, a melodious run leads back to the major mode, and Var. XV begins in extremely slow 6/8 time with a highly ornamental version of the Tune. Though nothing has been added to the framework, the Tune has become so enormously expanded by the slow time that I give a musical illustration of it below the original Tune to show the relation between them:

Ex. 1.

The whole theme, stated in this style with repeats, lasts fully a couple of minutes and fills several pages. The ornamentation becomes more and more brilliant, especially in that musical blank cheque, the second part of the theme; until some listeners might almost think it an open question whether Beethoven is taking quite seriously these great ladies whom he is portraying with such a bold technique. But Beethoven is too great a portrait painter to be unsympathetic even in satire; and there is no fundamental change of tone when in the coda he reverts harmonically to the plaintive rewriting of his Tune in C minor (as in Var. VI) while transforming it rhythmically to the following altogether new structure:

Ex. 2.

where you will see he gets the whole of the first part of the theme easily into the space of two bars. He hesitates for a long time on the dominant of this new key and strikes a solemn dramatic pause there.

Then the fugue begins quietly. Although it is on quite different lines from the fugue-passages in the Eroica finale, it foreshadows many salient features in the later work, being of course founded on the first four notes of the Bass which in later developments it turns upside down.

Ex. 3.

It also brings, as in the Eroica finale, the first phrase of the Tune into effective combination, reversing its accents in just the same surprising way as in the later work:

Ex. 4.

But, being exclusively a fugue, it has no room for those glorious episodes and complete variations which constitute half the bulk of the Eroica finale. However, it very clearly embodies the most glorious part of the whole scheme, in the culminating pause on the dominant followed by the final return of the Tune in slower time (andante) with its repeats varied and crowned with a last triumphant complete variation. After this the pianoforte work has little more to say. It concludes with the first notes of the Tune repeated in more and more rapid versions, like the last rotations of a spinning top. That is the way this great set of Pianoforte Variations ought to end. The Eroica finale uses the variation form only as one of many resources, and perhaps we shall enjoy its wonderful coda all the better for having now heard a work on the same material, where a simpler wind-up was right.

MÉHUL

CCXXXIII. OVERTURE, 'LE JEUNE SAGE ET LE VIEUX FOU'

Méhul is one of those composers whose fate is to be overrated by historians and underrated by musicians who approach his music keyed up to its historical reputation. Yet, music and all, he is one of the most sympathetic characters in the quiet backwaters of art. It is only his music which is a quiet backwater. His life extended from 1763 to 1817, and the one-act opera of which we are discussing the overture, was produced in the Year of Terror during which I forget what famous person's aunt continued her Tuesday afternoon receptions without interruption.

I do not know when I shall have leisure to write an essay on Méhul, for I see no opportunity of producing his most important works. He has been credited with powerful genius and an inexhaustible vein of melody. These compliments are so manifestly falsified by his works as to be positively slanderous. What chance would any of us have of appreciating Jane Austen if every primer of English literature inculcated that she was a powerful genius with an inexhaustible fertility in the invention of thrilling plots? On the other hand, I do not wish to imply any resemblance between Méhul and Jane Austen. He resembles no one but himself, and I have not space to indicate the range of his qualities here. The one thing for which he has been rightly praised is his instrumentation, which, though often primitive and perfunctory, is never for long without points of extraordinary interest. His chief misfortune is that his field of musical activity was opera, though I am not sure that he could have done better in other fields. Church music ought to have suited his style, and its opportunities in Paris throughout his career were as glorious as martyrs' crowns and angels' harps; but he missed them. He is said to have written forty-two operas, of which I have read fourteen. Sir Thomas Beecham, when I mentioned the subject to him some years ago, had read about twice as many, and probably by this time knows all the rest by heart. The only entire work of his which is revived nowadays is the Biblical opera *Joseph*, which I for my part consider rather his most characteristic than his most musical work.

The Overture to *Le Jeune Sage et le Vieux Fou* has recently found its way into concert repertoires for reasons which will be obvious to the listener. It is an excellent and exhilarating little piece, and contains by far the best music in the opera. None of the music, however, is as good as the libretto, which is among the most perfect one-act comedies I have ever read. It is by one Hoffman, presumably an Alsatian, who wrote a number of opera libretti, most of them very serious, for the French composers of those troubled times, his most famous libretto being that of Cherubini's *Médée*. Perhaps a faint threat of interruption to 'my aunt's Tuesday receptions' may be traced in the fact that the librettist's name is not mentioned on the title-page of the score of *Le Jeune Sage et le Vieux Fou*.

The overture begins with a solemn introduction, massive in rhythm and conception, but youthful in instrumentation,[1] and evidently representing the Good Young Man. The Giddy Greybeard is appropriately represented by a lively rondo, in which a fairly full orchestra comes into play, led off by bass instruments. Musical quotations are unnecessary, but the listener will appreciate the overture better, besides obtaining an unexpected sidelight on French music and literature during the Terror, if I outline the plot of the opera.

The curtain rises upon young Cliton in his dressing-gown, reading philosophy and distracted from his study by anxiety on account of his dissipated father, Merval. He decides that the only salvation is to marry his aged parent to some one with enough beauty and virtue to keep him straight; and he knows that a Suitable Young Person is about to call that very afternoon with her aunt. Merval, who had not come home till five o'clock that morning, enters humming the rondo-theme of the overture, and Cliton solemnly explains his plan. The old gentleman is so completely master of the situation as to know that Cliton's priggishness is far too innocent to be a bad sign. He also happens to know the charming Rose and her acidulated aunt, Elise, somewhat better than young Cliton is as yet capable of knowing anything but a book. Rose and Elise arrive. Conversational courtesies and operatic arias are exchanged, and the Young Philosopher's aria, in the style of the powerful introduction to the overture, discriminates diplomatically between the ephemeral charms of beauty as mentioned in the first stanza and those (with a bow to Aunt Elise) which remain to persons of mature years whose education has not been neglected.

Elise does not wish her niece to marry a prig, and has no intention herself of marrying a giddy-goat. When Merval says that

---

[1] I purposely refrained from giving particulars to the audience. The introduction, which should be conducted with Handel-Festival gestures, is scored for two flutes.

Cliton's character will change, she crushes him with the question, 'Has yours?'

Nevertheless Merval and Elise leave the young people together. Rose is as clever as Merval—that is to say, considerably cleverer than her aunt—and not only sees that a real person will, under suitable stimulus, some day emerge from young Cliton's chrysalis, but has with all maiden modesty already made up her mind to supply the stimulus. It therefore comes as a considerable shock to her when Cliton's solemn proposal ends with: 'Very well, to-morrow you will marry my father.' With superb presence of mind, she consents on one condition—that Cliton shall marry her aunt. This seems to Cliton, after a moment's reflection, to be a very sensible arrangement. His father needs all Rose's charms to keep him in order. Cliton himself is of steadier character, and the aunt will suffice for him. For a while, poor Rose does not feel her prospects to be particularly bright. She is, however, amused enough to tell this news, bursting with laughter, to her aunt, who instantly forms a totally different opinion of this most sensible young man's intelligence. (I have not space to indicate the excellent stagecraft by which the exits and entries in this one-room scene are managed.) The shrewd Merval, who perhaps may have read *Much Ado about Nothing*, contrives to put into his silly boy's head that Rose could allow herself to tell an old man what she could not tell his son. Then comes Aunt Elise, in full cry after her quarry. Cliton, not knowing that his original plans have leaked out through an indiscretion, finds her enthusiasm rather alarming, until he dutifully acquaints her with his intention of proposing to her niece. Her exit is abrupt, and Rose returns wondering what Cliton has said to put her aunt in such a temper. Cliton gravely explains that his plans, as previously sketched, must be altered. 'You love me; you told my father so, and you are incapable of lying. Hence it obviously follows that we must marry.' Merval brings Aunt Elise round in both the theatrical and the human sense, and the two couples are properly sorted in a happy finale.

MENDELSSOHN

CCXXXIV. OVERTURE, 'MELUSINE'

Mélusine was, as we are told by the *Encyclopædia Britannica*, the tutelary fairy of the house of Lusignan. In consequence of the kind of family quarrel that is to be expected with mixed marriages between fairies and mortals, she suffered on every Saturday from a change into serpent-form from the hips down. The condition was temporary and remediable by suitable bathing. But it was

necessary for her to find a husband who would never see her on
Saturdays. Raymond of Poitiers fulfilled this condition until he
yielded to the fatal curiosity of fairy-tale husbands, whereupon
she flew away in serpent-form,—*poussant des cris de Mélusine*, as
the proverb still runs. Henceforth her cries have always been
heard before the death of a Lusignan. This is the official legend,
but there seem to be other versions, in which Mélusine's trans-
formations were more fish-like than serpentine.

Although Mendelssohn had already written his wonderful
Hebrides Overture, he thought the *Melusine* Overture the best
thing he had ever done. He finished it in October 1833, and in
April 1834 he writes to his sister, Fanny Hensel, in answer to her
questions about its subject: 'Now attend. I'm cross! There you
go, asking me which tale you're to read! Well, how many are
there? And how many do I know, and don't you know the story
of the lovely Melusina? It's enough to make one crawl away and
disguise oneself in all manner of instrumental music without titles
when one's own sister (unnatural woman!) doesn't even approve
of the title. Perhaps you've really never heard of this beauteous
fish. However, when I consider how you might growl at me for
growling at you in April about a letter you wrote in February,
I will give in and be kind. I wrote this overture for an opera by
Conradin Kreutzer, which I heard about this time of year in the
Königstädter Theatre. The overture, I mean Kreutzer's, was
encored, and I disliked it quite particularly, and also the rest of
the opera, except Hähnel; but she was very engaging, especially
in one scene where she appeared in her fish-form and combed her
hair; whereupon I got a wish to make an overture which people
wouldn't encore, but would receive more inwardly, so I took
what I liked of the subject (and that corresponds exactly with
the fairy-tale), and, in short, the overture came into the world, and
that's its family history.'

In August 1834 he writes from Düsseldorf to his father that he
wanted to try his new Pianoforte Rondo in E flat from the proof-
copies, and summoned all the local musicians to rehearse it. As
they would have been offended at being paid for it, he gave them
a supper and made them as drunk as they liked. This, however,
was not the chief fun, but the Overture to *Melusine*, which he
also played for the first time, and which pleased him much. 'With
many pieces I know from the first bar that they'll sound well and
have some go in them, and so it was now, as soon as the clarinets
curled upwards in the first bar. The thing went badly, and yet
I had more pleasure than with many perfect performances and
went home in the evening feeling more cheerful than I had for
a long time. We played it three times, and after the third time,

directly after the last soft chord, the trumpets burst out in a flourish
with very comical effect. It was also nice when we were at supper,
and someone made a long speech ... and toasted me, whereupon
the trumpeters and drummer jumped up like mad and ran to their
instruments to make another flourish; and then I made a manly
speech, worthy of Sir Robert Peel, in which I preached unity and
Christian love and keeping time, and concluded with toasting the
progress of Düsseldorf music.'

The proceedings lasted till midnight, not without some quarrel-
someness by way of showing the effect of Mendelssohn's Peel-ine
oration.

Later, on 30 January 1836, Mendelssohn writes from Leipzig
to his sister that 'Many people here think *Melusine* is my best
overture; anyhow, it's the most intimate, but the rigmarole of the
Musikalische Zeitung about red coral and green sea-beasts and
magic castles and deep seas is all rubbish and astonishes me. All
the same, I'm going to take leave of water for some time, and
must look around for other prospects.' This last sentence refers
to his father's advice that he should 'hang upon a nail' the fairy-
tale subjects which had hitherto occupied him, and turn to something more serious. Perhaps the chief tragedy in Mendelssohn's
short career was that he took this advice.

The only weakness in the *Melusine* Overture is shown in the
half-phrase from the fifth to the eighth bar of its main theme—

Ex. 1.

a weakness for which the *locus classicus* is the Duetto in the *Songs
without Words*, where the inefficiency of the second clause shows
up fatally against the Aria 'With verdure clad' in Haydn's *Creation*.
The orthodox Mendelssohn-baiter glances at the first eight bars
of the *Melusine* Overture and inquires no farther. He does not
improve his taste by any so easy and summary a judgement. The
flaccid second clause is the only weakness in a composition very
perfect and distinguished and incomparably more serious than any
of Mendelssohn's later efforts to follow his father's deplorable
advice. The other themes are undistinguished; but weightier
themes would have spoiled the whole. The agitations and sorrows
of this piece are those of a fairy-tale, even if it be one that for some
persons concerned in it may end sadly. They are true and deep

(*innerlich*), as Mendelssohn always is when he is writing what he wants to write and not what he thinks he ought to write.

The opening clarinet-figure, whether it curls upwards, as in the theme, or downwards, as in the counterpoints, presumably represents the Saturday lower half of the lady, whether fish-like or serpentine or in the compromise of an eel. It may also represent waves of water, or, for all I know, the waves in which 'die Hähnel' combed her hair. None of these questions has the interest of good gossip, and for all they are worth Mendelssohn might just as well slink away from his *Rabenschwester's* questions and bury himself in absolute music. Far more interesting are the originality and freedom of the whole musical form, with its alternation between the beauty of calm water and fairy-tale terrors and woes. These more passionate elements are represented by the following pair of themes; conventional, but in the right conventions.

Ex. 2.

Ex. 3.

The work is undoubtedly not so deep as the *Hebrides* Overture or the music for *A Midsummer Night's Dream*; but Mendelssohn was not mistaken in thinking it one of his best. His father was mistaken in thinking that his son's fairy-tale world was a groove or in any danger of becoming a groove. Within that kingdom Mendelssohn was free and able to produce works far more distinct from each other than his 'more serious things'. You cannot drift from *Melusine* into the *Hebrides* or the *Midsummer Night's Dream* any more than you could drift into *Elijah*.

SCHUMANN

CCXXXV. OVERTURE, SCHERZO, AND FINALE, OP. 52

1 *Andante con moto: leading to Allegro.* 2 SCHERZO: *Vivo.* 3 FINALE: *Allegro molto vivace.*

This work was written at the same time as Schumann's First, Second, and Fourth Symphonies—that is to say, it was written in

1841 and revised, especially as to the finale, in 1845. Schumann is said to have thought of calling it a Sinfonietta. It is a pity that he did not finally decide on that title, for it precisely describes both the character and range of the work; whereas its present title implies something much less coherent, besides bringing in the quite irrelevant idea of an overture. There is, however, some colour for the title of 'overture' for the first movement, inasmuch as that movement is clearly influenced by a classic which we might as well revive, Cherubini's Overture to *Les Deux Journées*. Professor Niecks points out that that overture and other works of Cherubini impressed contemporaries as eminently romantic. What Berlioz says about Cherubini is not evidence; or, at all events, it is more evidential of Berlioz than of Cherubini. The *sprechender Bass*, the dramatic utterances of unaccompanied violoncellos and basses descending into the depths in impassioned recitative, is not the exclusive property of Berlioz and Liszt; nor are the sublime instrumental recitatives in Beethoven's Ninth Symphony its prototype. It was discovered by the earliest pioneers of instrumental and dramatic music in the seventeeth century; and in the Overture to *Les Deux Journées* Cherubini used it with a power which Beethoven could surpass only on the condition of seeing exactly what Cherubini meant by it.

The trouble with Cherubini is not that his style in opera is pedantic, but that his excellent histrionic devices are executed with an irreducible minimum of music. His style is theatrical in no vulgar sense. On the contrary, it is meticulously noble, if that is not a contradiction in terms; and so his romantic rhetoric impresses us now like stage scenery lying on the ground exposed to daylight. Schumann under the influence of Cherubini is more fortunate. Four bars of the introduction to his Sinfonietta, as I prefer to call it, compress into an epigram the whole romance of Cherubini's Overture to *Les Deux Journées*.

Ex. 1.

The allegro of the overture dances its way in Schumann's happiest vein of homage to Mendelssohn.

Ex. 2.

It drifts easily towards a second group in which the rhythms become broader and broader.

Ex. 3.

The intervention of material from the introduction, developing figures (*a*) and (*b*) at full speed, shows that Schumann intends to strike a dramatic note; but the continuation, after an abrupt pause—

Ex. 4.

proves that the movement of drama is precisely what his music cannot achieve, and is not really attempting. More clearly than in his larger symphonies, Schumann is building quasi-lyric epigrams into the musical equivalent of narrative or descriptive poetry that does not attempt the movement of either epic or drama. His Pegasus does not fly, but it ambles very comfortably and becomes more lyric than ever when the tempo becomes faster in the coda.

Ex. 5.

Our recovery from the anti-romantic reaction ought by now to allow us to treat this music as its boyish enthusiasm deserves. When Schumann was in fashion, every sentimental person proclaimed him as essentially manly, and therefore a composer in whose sentiment we could wallow without risk. But the truth is that Schumann is essentially boyish; and one paradoxical result is that he can afford to be crassly Mendelssohnian and to echo precisely Mendelssohn's weakest turns of phrase, because he is a naïve hero-worshipper. We must not sentimentalize Schumann. He has all the manly schoolboy's horror of any such tendency. On the other hand, nothing could be more detestably inartistic than to treat him with a schoolmasterly patronage or irony.

In the compact little scherzo—

Ex. 6.

and trio—

Ex. 7.

wind.   strings.

we have Schumann in his normal lyric element, with the normal
sectional forms of his *Phantasiestücke*. The coda alludes very
prettily to Ex. 2 from the first movement.

The finale moves imperturbably like the Red Queen crying,
'Faster, faster!' as she rushes with Alice ever onward under the
same tree in Looking-Glass Land. The first theme starts as a kind
of double fugue—

Ex. 8.
Upper theme.

which after three entries continues in lyric couplets or qua-
trains.

Ex. 9.

It drifts into the dominant, and there proceeds with new themes
which constitute a second group, the result being a sonata exposition in the sense in which Berlioz purports to have achieved such
a thing in the *Symphonie Fantastique* and the *Harold* Symphony;
but, as we shall see, Schumann shows that he is aware that he has
not achieved a classic example of the form. He directs that his
exposition should be repeated, and he proceeds to extract from its
last notes material for a discursive, but episodic, development—

Ex. 10.

Alice is decidedly short of breath; but she clings to the hand of the
flying Red Queen, while the four-bar phrases pursue their inex-
orable course. When Alice's second wind makes a quiet legato
possible, the second violin and viola convey fierce hints of an im-
minent return—

Ex. 11.

In due time the opening fugato (Ex. 8) returns in the home
tonic, and is cunningly expanded before proceeding with its lyric
continuation; and now Schumann proves that he knows that his

exposition had not the key-perspective of the sonata style, for he gives his whole second group unaltered in the dominant, reserving the home tonic for a coda which consists of a boyishly pompous augmentation of the whole main theme of its sequel (Exx. 8 and 9), and so brings one of his most delightful works to a punctual close. The boldness of keeping his whole second group in its original dominant shows a recovered mental energy far in advance of the convalescence which had proved manifestly not equal to carrying him through the finale of his Second Symphony.

BERLIOZ

CCXXXVI. 'SYMPHONIE FANTASTIQUE', OP. 14

1 REVÉRIES, PASSIONS. *Largo, leading to Allegro agitato e appassionato assai.* 2 UN BAL. *Valse. Allegro non troppo.* 3 SCÈNE AUX CHAMPS. *Adagio.* 4 MARCHE AU SUPPLICE. *Allegretto non troppo.* 5 SONGE D'UNE NUIT DE SABBAT. *Larghetto, leading to Allegro.*

Boiling oil awaits me for my irreverent treatment of Berlioz in the fourth volume of these Essays. Nevertheless, I claim to see a great deal more than his out-and-out admirers see in Berlioz, for they give me no sufficient evidence that they see enough in the art of music to measure anything so important as Berlioz's actual musical achievement. I have been blamed for 'repeating exploded fallacies' when I say that his musical technique is amateurish compared with that of his prose. My own literary claims are entirely amateurish, and I accept the judgement of such an acknowledged master of literature as W. E. Henley when he hails Berlioz as a fellow craftsman in prose. My judgement of Berlioz's technique is not based on the exploded fallacies of the musical critics of his day. Matthew Arnold thought that an institution such as the Académie Française was a safeguard against the weedy growth of *jugements saugrenus* and of projects that ought never to have been undertaken. Unfortunately French musical academicism is responsible for almost all that is most *saugrenu* in French music; and when it rises above that, it achieves the kind of perky slickness which deprives me of the last remains of my sense of fair play. So far, then, my sympathies are entirely with Berlioz. But I refuse to be bound by a statute of limitations which licenses me to tell brutal truths about the amateurishness of Gluck because he died in 1787, and forbids me to criticize Berlioz because he died in 1869 and is about to be canonized at his centenary. The canonizers (including the cleverest of all French academicians, Saint-Saëns) seem almost to wish to institute Berlioz's harmonic weaknesses into doctrines for the future.

But these weaknesses coincide suspiciously nearly with the commonest mistakes of a student with a defective ear for counterpoint. Schumann, the first and on the whole the most broadly and deeply sympathetic of Berlioz's early champions, pointed out that whenever Berlioz makes what seems manifestly a mistake every attempt to correct it substitutes for something characteristic something impossibly banal. I have never yet found a mistake in a student's composition of which this is not true. In a work of imagination every mistake (other than mere clerical errors or oversights) represents either a confusion of thought or an essentially impossible project. Hence any correction of it means abandoning at least half the thought or the whole essence of the project. Technical training consists mainly in the modest attempt to teach students to recognize and tackle the possibilities. One of the standard riddles of my class-room runs as follows:

Q. What is it which we all wish to learn from the Great Masters, and why can we never learn it?

A. How to get out of a hole: because they never get into one.

There is not sufficient reason for believing that the most promising student is the one who never gets into a hole; but there is still less reason for supposing that every student who spends all his time getting into holes is a Berlioz. It has been suggested that it was a pity Cherubini did not grant Berlioz's wish for the professorship of harmony. Cherubini's own academicism was bad enough in all conscience; but a traditional academic tyranny would be freedom itself compared with that of a composer who proclaimed a crusade against appoggiaturas (which is like proclaiming a crusade against all figures of speech), and who professed an utter detestation of all sixteenth-century polyphony, all Bach, all polyphonic organ music, and, in fact, everything that he would not have written himself. Berlioz's most violent aversion was Wagner. Whatever may be said of his harmonic theories, they were anything but advanced.

Grammatical rules can be very silly; perhaps sillier in music than in literature, because in spoken languages they are demonstrable questions of usage, whereas in music they are questions of sound, and hence of taste. It is possible that a split infinitive may be less illiterate than the only circumlocution that can be devised to avoid it; and it is possible that an incorrect doubled leading-note may not 'tickle like cake-crumbs in bed'. But the least pedantic of critics will agree with Mr. Punch that the English infinitive was racked beyond human endurance by the sonnet which began

To with the lark and with the sun arise—

And so perhaps it is as well that Berlioz gave warning in the very first two bars of the *Symphonie Fantastique* that he did not feel doubled leading-notes as the Real Princess in the fairy-tale felt the pea under a mountain of bed-clothes.

The *Symphonie Fantastique* has the advantage, rare in Berlioz's greater works, of illustrating a programme of his own invention. We are thus not vexed by the effort to trace any evidence of his attention to Shakespeare (as in *Roméo et Juliet, avec le dénouement de Garrick*) or to Byron, as in *Harold en Italie*, which consists exclusively of scenes not described by Byron: nor need we speculate, as in the case of his *Grande Messe des Morts* and *Te Deum*, about his attitude to religion, or about any other things which he had the statesmanship to keep to himself.

Here is his own account of the *Symphonie Fantastique*, interspersed with the few musical quotations and supplementary remarks necessary or provocative.

NOTICE

The following programme should be distributed among the audience whenever the *Symphonie Fantastique* is performed dramatically, that is to say, followed by the Monodrama of *Lélio*, which ends it and completes the *Episode de la vie d'un artiste*. In that case the orchestra is invisible and placed on the stage of a theatre with lowered curtain.

Nothing will induce me to expose Berlioz by any such scheme, nor will I discount, by any description of *Lélio*, the effect the *Symphonie Fantastique* ought to produce. There are good things in *Lélio*, but its scheme is supremely absurd and its final fantasia on Shakespeare's *Tempest* is beyond redemption by the canonizers of Berlioz.

When the Symphony is played alone in a concert this arrangement is unnecessary: indeed, even the distribution of the programme is not absolutely essential so long as the titles of the five movements are set forth; for the author hopes that the Symphony can provide its own musical interest independently of any dramatic intention.

A very just claim, sometimes ignored by the canonizers of Berlioz. Nevertheless, his 'programme' is here a very considerable help to the understanding of his music, and no analysis, nor any score, however miniature, should omit it.

PROGRAMME OF THE SYMPHONY

A young musician of morbid sensibility and ardent imagination is in love, and has poisoned himself with opium in a fit of desperation. Not having taken a lethal dose, he falls into a long sleep in which he has the strangest dreams, wherein his feelings, sentiments, and memories are translated by his sick brain into musical ideas and figures. The beloved woman herself has become a melody which he finds and hears everywhere as an *Idée fixe*.

First Movement. Reveries, Passions.

First he remembers the uneasiness of mind, the aimless passions, the baseless depressions and elations which he felt—

Ex. 1.

[In C minor. Later, at the same pitch, harmonized in E flat.]

before he saw the object of his adoration—

Ex. 2.

The *Idée fixe*.

then the volcanic love which she instantly inspired in him, his delirious agonies, his jealous rages, his recovered love, his consolations of religion.

Ex. 2 gives the whole of the *Idée fixe*. Other details and phases are easily followed without too meticulous an attention to the 'programme'. The quiet end represents the consolations of religion, by several kinds of 'amen' chords.

Second Movement. A Ball.

He meets his beloved at a ball in the midst of the tumult of a brilliant festival.

The *Idée fixe* enters as a middle episode, and reappears as a lingering farewell in a quiet passage in the coda.

Third Movement. Pastoral Scene.

On a summer evening in the country he hears two shepherds [presumably a lad and a lass] playing a *Ranz des Vaches* in dialogue.

This pastoral duet, the place, the gentle sound of wind in the trees, a few recently conceived grounds of hope, all tend to give a new calm to his heart and a brighter colour to his thoughts.

But She [the *Idée fixe*] appears again. His heart misses a beat; he is troubled by grievous forebodings. What if she should deceive him? . . .

One of the shepherds resumes his simple lay; the other does not answer. The sun sets. Distant thunder. Solitude. Silence.

Fourth Movement. March to Execution.

He dreams that he has killed his beloved; that he is condemned to death, and led to the place of execution. The procession moves to a march, now gloomy and wild—

Ex. 7.

—now brilliant and grand—

Ex. 8.

during which the dull sound of heavy footsteps follows abruptly upon the noisiest outbursts.

Berlioz's prize modulation, which he implores the orchestral players not to 'correct', is the following juxtaposition of the chords of D flat and G minor.

Ex. 9.

At last the *Idée fixe* reappears for a moment, as a last thought of love, cut short by the stroke of death.

Fifth Movement. Dream of a Witches' Sabbath.

[Elsewhere described by Berlioz as the dream of a cut-off head.]
He finds himself in a Witches' Sabbath, in the midst of a frightful crowd of ghosts, sorcerers, and all manner of monsters assisting at his entombment. Weird noises, groans, bursts of laughter, distant cries echoed by others. The Beloved Melody enters again, but it has lost its noble modesty; it has become a vulgar dance-tune, trivial and grotesque. SHE has come to the Witches' Sabbath.

The *Idée fixe* on an E flat clarinet (or broomstick).

Ex. 10.

&c. through the
whole extent of Ex. 2.

Roars of joy at her arrival. She joins in the devilish orgies. Funeral bells, parody of the Dies Irae [one of the grandest of all plain-chants].

Ex. 11.
Dies Irae.

repeated in quicker notes until it becomes a jig.

Round-dance of the witches.

La *Ronde du Sabbat* et la *Dies Irae* ensemble.

And so Berlioz, for all his hatred of what the academic musicians taught him, really lets himself go and best displays his freedom as a composer when he is building up long rounds as in the *Scène aux champs* (Ex. 5) and fugues, as upon Ex. 12, which swings along spendidly; and his proudest climaxes are wholesale combinations which he naïvely advertises as such. He is big enough to stand our poking a little fun at him; and I am sorry if the out-and-out Berliozians are not.

CCXXXVII. OVERTURE, 'LE CORSAIR'

Berlioz has been officially pronounced by himself and others to be an inveterate writer of programme music. Every instrumental piece paints a picture, and every picture tells a story; and the greatest story-teller is Berlioz himself. When we turn to the alleged sources of his inspiration, the educational value in his propaganda is revealed as a stimulus to the study of literature for literature's sake. We need not trouble to assume that Berlioz's *Corsair* can be any other than Byron's. Byron is out of fashion nowadays, and I seldom read poetry, because I find that poetry must be read aloud, and that I cannot long continue to read aloud in a room whence all but I have fled. Berlioz has now twice induced me to read works of Byron—viz. *Childe Harold's Pilgrimage* and *The Corsair*—which otherwise I might have failed to read; and I can proudly claim now to have read them for their own sake, since the light they throw upon Berlioz's music is nil. Byron's Corsair is, of course, Byron himself, mythically wicked, sinister, and diabolically noble. Berlioz himself is a Brocken spectre mas-

querading as Byron upon a cloud-scape of abstract orchestration
which is for him the one solid reality among the illusions of what
Kipling has somewhere described as the child that has hit its head
against the bad, wicked table. Gigantic as the Brocken spectre is,
Berlioz himself is greater than Byron. He is not, perhaps, as great
as Cervantes, but he is as great as Don Quixote. Only very silly
people will take him seriously, but they are not as silly as the people
who don't.

The Overture to *Le Corsair* is as salt a sea-piece as has ever been
written. Wagner, we are told, was a good enough sailor to derive
inspiration by experience for his Overture to *The Flying Dutchman*.
Turner, we are told, lashed himself to the mast of a fishing vessel
in order to make sketches at sea during a storm. I believe Berlioz
tells some similar story about himself. If not, he ought to have done
so. The duty of the analysis writer will have been done if these hints
will project the imagination of the audience into the composite
mind of Berlioz-Wagner-Turner-Byron lashed to the broken mast
of a fishing vessel foundering in a gale while we listen in comfort to
this saline music. Of the parting of Conrad and Medora, Francis
Jeffrey has said: 'We do not know anything in poetry more beautiful
or touching than this picture'; and my childhood memories
are dominated by an engraving of this subject in which the
figures of Conrad and Medora are hardly noticeable in a vast
Elysian landscape by John Martin, in whose heyday Turner was
as invisible as Wagner in the glare of Meyerbeer, but whose more
favourite subjects were the destruction of towered cities by the
letter Z descending from lurid skies. There can be little doubt
that the slow theme in A flat near the beginning of Berlioz's Overture is inspired by the parting of Conrad and Medora. It 'registers'
feminine chastity and tenderness, in much the same universal
formulas as the first feminine theme in Berlioz's *Roméo et Juliette*.

Ex. 1.

Adagio sostenuto.

Sea breezes and sea foam are suggested to me and other naïve
listeners by the impetuous opening, which I do not quote. I cannot identify anything else in the overture with any special features
in Byron's *Corsair*. Byron has one other feminine character, Gulnare, chief jewel of the Harem of the Pacha Seyd, from whose
fetters she heroically rescues the captive Conrad, whose constancy
to his Medora is confirmed by his horror at discovering that Gulnare has slain her detestable lord and master as part of the procedure of his rescue. His own countless murders in the sacred cause

of piracy write no wrinkle on his azure brow. Eventually he finds
his Medora dead and her castle in ruins. I cannot trace any of
these events in Berlioz's entirely brilliant overture, and have not
the slightest idea of what Byronic subjects, other than generalized
brilliance, are represented by the main theme into which the
breezy elements settle.

Ex. 2.

Eminent critics (the epithet is as essential as 'indefatigable' to
secretaries) are warned against imputing to deficiency of ensemble
Berlioz's discovery that this theme, like any theme that will kindly
stay long enough on one arpeggio, goes into canon at one beat's
distance. Like most of his latest works, such as the *Harold* Symphony, the *Corsair* Overture was revised from things drafted in his
Conservatoire days, when human nature revolted against the crass
stupidity of his counterpoint masters, and at the same time
snatched at every opportunity of displaying the canonic accom-
plishments they purported to teach. Ex. 2 eventually appears
jauntily in the dominant as a soprano melody. But I cannot find
any feminine element to correspond to the heroic Gulnare. Perhaps she shocked Berlioz even more than she shocked the pirate
and Byron.

The processes that may be academically described as development are dominated by Ex. 1, thus giving the pirate credit for his
constancy to Medora. But, on the whole, it is dangerous to accuse
Berlioz of attention to his programme.

I do not know why *Le Corsair* is not more often played. To me
it is one of Berlioz's most attractive works. Like all of them, it
arouses my irreverence, and my fiercest resentment against any
one who dares to say a word against it. Berlioz must have been
even more than usually proud of the harmonic originality of his
final cadence—

Ex. 3.

and here he commands the complete sympathy of any one who can
appreciate good harmony.

CCXXXVIII. OVERTURE, 'BÉATRICE ET BÉNÉDICT'

Berlioz's *Béatrice et Bénédict* consists of *Much Ado about Nothing* without the Ado.

Hero and Claudio are the serious lovers; and they both display a decorous melancholy without being troubled by the Don John plot. This is to the advantage of Claudio, of whom Berlioz lets us know nothing worse than that he is a lovesick hero returned safely from a singularly bloodless war. As for Hero, somebody has got to be serious, to give the opera a chance for slow tempi. The main concern of the opera is the cat-and-dog bickerings of Beatrice and Benedick (it would be pedantry to expect a Parisian, to say nothing of a Gascon, to distinguish between Benedick and Bénédict, when no Parisian ever got nearer to the name of Franz Liszt than 'Monsieur Lits'), and the sudden conversion of the two into lovers when certain minor characters arrange that they shall overhear conversations about the evidently true state of their affections.

As this does not give enough material for a two-act opera, Berlioz has not only a number of Sicilian dances and choruses as *divertissements*, but introduces a *maestro*, of the appropriate name of Somarone, who in honour of Claudio and Hero rehearses an asinine epithalamium in a form which Berlioz's training at the Paris Conservatoire led him to believe was a possible parody of a sixteenth-century madrigal. Maestro Somarone, finding that the composition lacks unction as it stands, sketches with masterly rapidity an extra oboe obbligato which worms and warbles its way through the final performance with the intended comic effect. The text of the madrigal begins appropriately with *Mourez, tendres époux*, which causes the dear old Duke to inquire why the happy couple should die just yet. He is duly informed that this is an expression characteristic of the higher orders of poetry, and the public is informed in an aside that His Highness is a Philistine and a bourgeois.

Berlioz, having thus spent twenty minutes in venting his nasty temper on the subject of all that he had been taught at the Paris Conservatoire by poor old curmudgeon Cherubini, and incidentally in revealing that master's dismal lack of genuine sixteenth-century culture, is free to devote the rest of his opera to very pretty music, of which the overture is an excellent example. It has three contrasted themes, of which the first is stated in triple time in what proves to be an introduction.

Ex. 1.

Allegro scherzando.

The exposition of this is interrupted by an excerpt from the aria in which Béatrice finds herself in love.

Il m'en sou-vient, Il m'en sou-vient le jour du dé - part de l'ar-

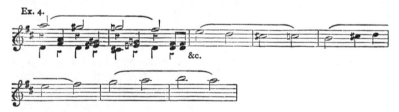

- mé - e,   Je ne pus m'ex-pli - quer   L'é - tran - ge sen - ti - ment,
&c.

Then the main movement of the overture begins. It is in compact sonata form with Ex. 1 turned into allabreve time as its main theme, a brassy transition-theme—

and a short second group in the dominant consisting chiefly of a theme in minims—

which I am not able to associate with anything particular in the opera, though there are passages more or less resembling it.

I do not know why this Overture is not more often played; nor, indeed, why the whole opera is not better known. Perhaps it is because Berlioz, like Liszt, took pains to give himself a reputation as a devil-worshipper. Most of his contemporaries had already come to think that the main purposes of a Black Mass were those of sensational fiction; but it was long before they came to realize that the writers of sensational fiction are for the most part the most respectable and amiable of persons. *Dulce est desipere in loco*, and the Overture to *Béatrice et Bénédict* is excellent fooling, and neither more nor less scholarly than the fooling of the persons it describes

CCXXXIX. A FURTHER NOTE ON BRAHMS'S TRAGIC OVERTURE (OP. 81)

It is some time since Brahms has definitely come into his own and escaped from the dangerous championship of the anti-Wagnerian Brahmsian, as well as from the helpless fulminations of the people whose only approach to music is through the theatre and literature. But certain features of Brahms's style still seem to lie beyond the range of current criticism. In recent judgements of the Tragic Overture, I cannot trace the slightest progress in intelligence since the days when it was a new work. My analysis of it, as issued by me at Reid Concerts, and as now published by the Oxford University Press (*Essays in Musical Analysis*, Vol. II, p. 151), began with a discussion of the meaning of tragedy in music and literature. This was rash. I was as helpless as Huckleberry Finn arguing with Jim the nigger. Cats have a right to talk like cats; but Frenchmen, being men, ought to talk like other people. And so Brahms ought to write Russian music. Let's begin again on a clean slate.

Ex. 1.

The main difficulty in appreciating Brahms's right to call this greatest of his orchestral movements tragic seems to me to lie in current ignorance of the meaning of his language. In Ex. 1, the two figures marked (*e*) and (*f*) are the real stumbling-blocks to most critics and many conductors. They are lively figures, and the treatment of fig. (*e*) in the *più moderato* development is child-like. In *Coriolanus*, the boy Marcus makes us laugh at one of the tensest moments of the drama. We have enough faith in Shakespeare to believe that this is not an oversight, and we do not insist upon having the boy represented with a Roman nose as developed as that of his father. Current notions of tragic values in music are less advanced.

The other unappreciated aspect of Brahms's style concerns his most characteristic ruminating passages: such things as the development of the finale of the Second Symphony, and almost the whole of the finale of the C minor Pianoforte Quartet. There was a time when, under the guidance of John Hullah, Bach was regarded as a monumental composer with a style entirely devoid of expression, but 'unique', as Hullah said, 'like the Pyramids, in the quality of being satisfactory'. Many of us can recollect with affection some dutiful and venerable music-lover who, at the prospect of listening to Bach, would say 'Yes, Bach is so SATISFACTORY' before closing her eyes. It is an unfortunate fact that Brahms's profoundest ruminating developments and episodes are inevitably woven in a close contrapuntal texture which is very interesting to analyse and very much like the most elaborate textures of Bach. Experience has taught me simply to withhold the analysis of such passages altogether so long as the view prevails that all such things are inherently pedantic. It is, of course, foolish to suppose ingenuity to be more than a practical necessity for the construction of such passages. But it is worse than childish to suppose that the necessary ingenuity is a sign of pedantry.

This prejudice has now attained such a vogue that it has become worse than the silliness of the listener and critic who can understand music only in terms of literary and pictorial illustration. All good musicians hate the practice of illustrating purely instrumental music by other objects, and we musicians have even acquired an habitual resentment against any tendency to lay stress upon the musical illustration of words, even when the words or dramatic actions are essential to the very existence of the music. I have often protested against the habit of digesting Beethoven with the aid of a diet of Carlyle's *French Revolution* relieved by doses of *The Scarlet Pimpernel*; but there comes a point when the persistent decrying of such a work as Brahms's Tragic Overture must be met by propaganda more popular than an attempt to explain pure music to people who greatly prefer it impure. I find that the middle part of the overture is considered unintelligibly dry, and that many conductors have grave doubts as to whether Brahms can possibly have meant it to be taken twice as slow as the rest. Perhaps listeners so prejudiced may get some idea of what I take to be Brahms's intention if they will remind themselves of the character of Grizel in *Sentimental Tommy*, with particular reference to the passages where she is described as persistently prying upon the laying-out of a corpse because she knows that her outcast mother, the 'painted lady', is dying, and that she herself had better practise betimes a task in which she does not wish for the help of the scornful. I had not read *Sentimental Tommy* when I had the good fortune to get my first impressions of the Tragic Overture from a perfect performance under Steinbach at Meiningen in 1899; but I was then deeply impressed by the mysterious purposefulness of its quiet

development and the overpowering pathos of its musical consequences in the recapitulation. Joachim had all the absolute
musician's horror of gratuitous literary illustration, but Brahms did
not snub him for comparing the finale of the Third Symphony with
the story of Hero and Leander; and I do not think, if I had been
able to show Brahms this passage in *Sentimental Tommy*, that he
would have snubbed me. I had forgotten all about it when I
wrote of the frightened child whose thought was 'what ought
I to do?'

VERDI

CCXL. 'STABAT MATER', FOR CHORUS AND ORCHESTRA

Of the Four Sacred Pieces which constitute Verdi's last work, the
Stabat Mater is the most important and the most perfect. The *Te
Deum* is a little more voluminous, but does not achieve the consistency of style shown in the *Stabat Mater*, nor is it so unquestionably beautiful in conception, though it is very impressive. To
complain that either work is theatrical or unecclesiastical is as
relevant as the discovery that it is not only foreign but positively
un-English. Verdi at eighty was no more aware than Verdi at
thirty that music could be anything but theatrical. He was hardly
aware that it could be theatrical. In Italy an Englishman, and *a
fortiori* a Scot, may be known by his tendency to remark that 'it is
a fine day'. This puzzles the native, who gets his bad weather in
very effective doses when it does come, but whose fine days are
just 'days'. The strangest thing about the inveterately theatrical
Verdi is that he had a profound love of Palestrina; and the strangest thing about Verdi's *Stabat Mater* is that in spirit and also in
form it resembles Palestrina's *Stabat Mater* more than any other
setting of that poem, though the more you study it the more
its at first sight glaring difference from the Verdi of *Trovatore*
vanishes.

The spirit of the work is not a matter of language. The style of
the stage is not ecclesiastical. The Latin of St. Jacopo di Todi is
not classical. And there we may leave the stylistic criticism of
words and music. Questions of form and method are less jejune.
The poem falls into two parts, a meditation and a prayer. The
meditation is a series of the simplest possible mental pictures of the
Virgin Mother standing by the Cross; the prayer is for a share in
her sorrows, with the hope of Paradise after death. Tolstoy's three
staretsi hardly attained a more simple saintliness. But the
simplicity itself is mystical, though the substance is concrete and

emotional, with none of the close-packed parables and metaphors of the *Pange lingua*. Palestrina's setting is one of the simplest compositions in the world, as simple as Bach's Chromatic Fantasia, the purest cloud-scape in the world of harmony, without even a flight of birds to show the scale of its mighty perspective. The rhythm is that of the quantities of the words; there is no polyphony and no themes. Translate the tonality from free Dorian to modern minor and major with unlimited range of key; add a full Italian orchestra with Italian traditions of scoring, grandiose and whole-sale in method, yet refined by the experience of an octogenarian; and the analysis of Palestrina's *Stabat Mater* will fit Verdi's better than you might expect. Palestrina's Dorian mode keeps his strange harmonies together. Verdi's modulations are instinctively balanced around the G minor of his beginning and end. His last notes are those to which the three words 'Stabat Mater dolorosa' are set at the beginning; otherwise there is no theme to hold the work to-gether. His enormous talent for composition enabled him in his earlier works to give life to the crudest schemes of rhythm and phrasing; and now it enables him to make the lines of the poem roll on in their groups of three like a planet in its orbit. He does not overburden his declamation with grammatical analysis; for example, he is content to set 'Me sentire vim doloris' as a complete line without running on to the word 'fac', which is needed to com-plete the sense; but he does not, like Pergolese, make it impossible to understand by repeating the line again and again and then set-ting 'fac ut tecum lugeam' as an entirely separate proposition. In short, he is neither conventional nor pedantic: he knows how words actually are spoken and does not argue, like Dr. Johnson, that a negative commandment such as 'Thou shalt not steal' should stress the word 'not', in defiance of the plain fact that in common speech 'shalt not' has become 'shan't'.

TCHAIKOVSKY

CCXLI. SYMPHONY IN E MINOR, NO. 5, OP. 64

1 *Andante, leading to Allegro con anima.* 2 *Andante cantabile, con alcuna licenza.* 3 *Valse. Allegro moderato.* 4 *Finale. Andante maestoso, leading to Allegro vivace.*

It cannot be too often pointed out that the duty of the writer of programme notes is that of counsel for the defence. Whatever the discerning critic may find to say against a composition, the pro-gramme writer has no business to say anything that interferes with the listener's enjoyment of the music; but he may be guided by times and seasons. When the work is so new and strange that responsible opinions may differ as to its strong and weak points, the analyst is justified in taking the strongest defensive line, limited only by carefully avoiding any attack upon music of other tendencies.

At the time of Brahms's death in 1897, Tchaikovsky was at the height of his popularity, and his own recent death was shrouded in tragic mystery. Even the 'Brahminen' were remarkably timid in their obituary estimate of Brahms, and it was the correct thing to say that his symphonies were eclipsed by Tchaikovsky's. Of course they were, for they were not light music; and with this awful statement I have perhaps more than redressed the balance that I find myself to have disturbed by my high and sincere praise of Tchaikovsky's Pathetic Symphony. Now that my analyses have been collected in book form, the limitations of a counsel for the defence become manifest. The reader, no longer so conscious of the needs of the concert-goer, is apt to assume that I am still talking of the highest classical values, when I am merely stating the legitimate case for other music which is conspicuously the best of its kind. I have said nothing in praise of the Pathetic Symphony which I wish to retract. Nor have I given any grounds for supposing that I think its forms more than successful according to their lights. But I should not have helped the listener by introducing what I take to be Tchaikovsky's best work with an air of damaging patronage. If in 1907 a programme writer had dared to insinuate that Tchaikovsky was primarily a writer of light music and that his tragedy was melodrama, the only effect would have been to excite the exultant fury of the 'Brahminen' against the numerically overwhelming opposition of all more persuasive and popular critics. The controversy would have soared to the Empyrean of that region which the Germans have somehow failed to designate by the name of *Heibrau*, and everybody would have been made uncomfortable; though not nearly so uncomfortable as Brahms and Tchaikovsky would have been in the presence of each other.

To-day the situation is different. The *Heibrauen* do not seem clear as to the distinction between a writer of deservedly popular music and a humbug. At all events, the distinction becomes easier to appreciate when the music is at least a hundred years old. No sensible person is nowadays distressed at seeing a case made out for Weber; and no responsible person at this time of day wants to make out a case for Meyerbeer, though his arch-enemy, Wagner, qualified his fiercest denunciations by a most generous praise of the end of the fourth act of *Les Huguenots*. A clear distinction between good music and bad ought to be absolute for responsible persons. The distinction between bad good music and good bad

music is an excellent conversational topic for talkers who can keep
their tempers, but I have never ventured to prescribe it as a subject
for students' essays. Nor do my duties as counsel for defence
compel me to say anything further that can interfere with the
listener's enjoyment of Tchaikovsky's Fifth Symphony. I hope
all listeners will be able to enjoy the whole of it. Confession and
avoidance, however, can remove a serious obstacle to their enjoyment of the finale. I have said of the Pathetic Symphony that its
slow finale 'is a stroke of genius which solves all the artistic problems that have proved most baffling to symphonic writers since
Beethoven'. The statement has shocked some people almost as
much as if I had said that it was the greatest finale since Beethoven;
but the problems I refer to are simply the problems of getting up
any sense of movement in a finale at all; and I am afraid that my
locus classicus for impotence in that matter is the finale of Tchaikovsky's Fifth Symphony. If the composer had intended to
produce the nightmare sensation, or the Alice-and-Red-Queen
sensation, of running faster and faster while remaining rooted to
the spot, he might have been said to have achieved his aim here;
but the melancholy fact remains that this finale resembles all other
compositions in which the vitally necessary problem of movement
has simply not occurred to the composer at all. I have been
generously praised for my defence of Bruckner, whose popularity,
now at best-seller height in Germany and Austria, has not yet
begun in England; and, that being so, nobody has objected to my
saying frankly that you must not expect Bruckner to make a finale
'go'. But the popular Tchaikovsky is in worse case than Bruckner,
for he evidently expects his finales to 'go', and neither the naïve
listener, nor the still more naïve *Heibrau*, can at this time of day
be helped by an analysis that leaves it to him to discover the fact
that Tchaikovsky's finale wants to go and cannot.

One sometimes encounters the view that Tchaikovsky's Fifth
Symphony is finer than the *Pathétique*, on the ground that it has
fewer 'tricks'. Tchaikovsky's orchestration is undoubtedly vivid,
and the salient features of the Pathetic Symphony are specially
ingenious. I don't know if anything else in the Pathetic Symphony
is to be called 'tricks'; but if tricks are good tricks, I prefer to have
as many of them as possible, and I am not disinclined to call them
ideas. So now let us see how many ideas we can find in this Fifth
Symphony, and let no *Heibrau* persuade us to throw the baby out
with the bath-water.

The introduction sets forth a dour melody which I leave
to musical folk-lorists to put into the right pigeon-hole among
their Russian folk-songs, premising only that Tchaikovsky was
abundantly capable of inventing it himself.

Ex. 1.

It appears at dramatic points in later movements of the Symphony, and may be regarded as its motto.

The allegro begins with an equally lyric theme—

Ex. 2.

which builds up by a crescendo of repetitions to a big tutti which eventually effects a transition to dramatic action. Great harmonic distinction is given to this theme by its first note. Those who misremember it as B will learn a useful lesson in style when they come to notice that this note is C and not B.

From this tune the music rouses itself to fluent dramatic action, in the course of which a new incident—

Ex. 3.

seems to be about to make a transition; but this is eventually effected by Ex. 2.

From this the transition is prompt, and a new theme appears in the dominant minor.

Ex. 4.

This shapes itself as the first member of a second group, which soon changes its key to the unusual region of D major, the flat seventh, where a new pair of themes is given, of which the first—

Ex. 5.

is remarkable for the colour of the wind chords, while the second—

Ex. 6.

introduces a melting cantabile in a Brahmsish cross-rhythm. The direction 'molto più tranquillo' has led to a tradition that pulls this passage entirely out of relation to the main tempo, but Tchaikovsky adds a metronome mark ($\downarrow$. = 92) which leaves it well in touch with the rest. His exaggerated markings indicate nerves rasped by the inattention of conductors and players to ordinary nuances. Like most of such nervous reactions they defeat their object; and later editors make matters worse by adding more marks. Ex. 6 leads to a passionate climax in which the figure of Ex. 2 appears, after which Ex. 5 brings the exposition to a triumphant end.

The sounds of triumph fade away and pass into a contrapuntal development of the figures of Exx. 1 and 5, modulating through dark keys. Suddenly a storm bursts out on the transition theme (Ex. 3). Then Ex. 4 is developed in combination with other figures. At no immoderate length another climax is reached, and a return is made, through an outlying region of G minor, into the home tonic with a very impressive sudden diminuendo. The bassoon, an instrument much honoured and sometimes sorely tried in this symphony, brings back the main theme (Ex. 2) at exactly the right moment.

The recapitulation is quite regular, B minor being replaced by C sharp minor, which leads to the home tonic.

The coda works up Ex. 2 in a lively crescendo, the climax of which initiates a basso ostinato on the notes E, D, C, B, which persists for 28 repetitions to within 8 bars of the end, while Ex. 2 is almost as obstinate in the treble. The diminuendo reaches a darkness almost as Cimmerian as those in the Pathetic Symphony. But it would be a mistake to impute any deep psychic gloom to this excellent and pleasantly sardonic first movement, or indeed to any part of this symphony.

The andante begins with 8 bars of hymn-like chords which, starting as if in B minor, swing round to D major, the key of the second group in the first movement. These chords might well have become an important theme, or at least a canto fermo; but they are not heard again, their sole function being this swing from B minor to D. They drift into an accompaniment to a broad melody given out by the first horn.

Ex. 7.

From this arises an auxiliary theme in the bright key of F sharp major.

Ex. 8.

This is the chief topic of the most impassioned climaxes in this movement.

A middle episode, 'moderato con anima', modulating widely, begins in F sharp minor with the following theme—

Ex. 9.

At its climax the home dominant is reached, and the motto theme (Ex. 1) appears with great emphasis in a significant new position.

One of the most famous of all Tchaikovsky's rhetorical strokes is the short pause and swinging pizzicato chords which follow this by way of return to the main theme (Ex. 7), which is now adorned by rhythmic imitations in the oboe and other wind instruments.

The final climax of the movement concerns itself chiefly with Ex. 8. Towards the end the fateful motto theme intervenes thunderously in a new position. After this the rest of the movement is an impressive dying away on the topic of Ex. 7.

The graceful valse which does duty for scherzo can be enjoyed without the aid of quotations. A notorious passage for the bassoon owes most of its atrocious difficulty to the assumption that Tchaikovsky intends it to be brilliant. I see no reason to doubt that his intention is rather that it should be the one note of passion in an otherwise indolently graceful movement; and, in particular, that it should thus enhance the contrast afforded by the lively trio with its spiccato runs. In the coda the ghost of Ex. 1 appears dimly.

By way of introduction to the finale, Ex. 1 presents itself very much in the flesh and in majestic tonic major. It alternates with a new chord theme—

Ex. 10.

which introduces darker keys (G major in relation to E minor), and eventually causes the bass to settle upon G, and to remain there not only while the introduction dies away, but also while the following self-repeating theme of an allegro vivace breaks through—

Ex. 11.

I have already expressed my doubt as to whether Tchaikovsky intends his finale to give an impression of struggling vainly to achieve flight, but perhaps the listener will enjoy it best if he assumes that to be the composer's intention. New figures, such as—

Ex. 12.

do not release us from the rhythmic bondage of the old themes with which they combine, and their presence in the bass does not long prevent the bass from subsiding into vast pedal points.

Ex. 13.

When at last a new cantabile appears as the chief member of the second group, it enters over an ostinato that has already persisted for a long time, and is going to persist much longer. Again we find ourselves in the D major characteristic of the work.

Ex. 14.

By way of change of movement, the motto theme (Ex. 1) bursts out in full majesty without slackening the tempo, and its second figure is ingeniously paraphrased in terms of Ex. 11, thus initiating a development in which Ex. 13 stalks on its way, sometimes below, and sometimes above, the ostinato figure derived from the first notes of Ex. 11.

At last an impressive diminuendo with fine modulations reduces fig. (*b*) to repeated chords, while the other ostinato, fig. (*a*), discovers that it has been representing the home tonic for a long time. Then a recapitulation begins, Ex. 11 bursting out suddenly as bass to a new theme. The other materials follow in more or less their original sequence, the second group answering its former D major by the new and bold colour of F sharp major. This is brought round to the home dominant, on which the rhythm, but not at first the actual theme, of Ex. 1 asserts itself. Its actual appearance as a theme is carefully deferred until a grand climax of themeless chords has duly prepared us for a triumphal march ('moderato assai e molto maestoso') in the major. As such, with new counter-points, Ex. 1 now displays itself at leisure, with accompaniments of increasing brilliancy. Then there is a return to presto, where a further coda deals with Exx. 12 and 13.

But the last word of the symphony is concerned with neither the issues of the finale nor the motto theme, but with the main theme of the first movement (Ex. 2) in grandiose major and unqualified cheerfulness.

My own conclusion about Tchaikovsky's Fifth Symphony is that great injustice to its intentions results from regarding it as in any way foreshadowing the Pathetic Symphony. Like all Tchaikovsky's works, it is highly coloured; and a critic who should call it restrained would be in evident medical need of restraint himself; but the first three movements are in well-proportioned orthodox form, and my general impression of this symphony is that from first to last Tchaikovsky, though I have never been able to impute to him a sense of humour, is thoroughly enjoying himself. And I don't see why we shouldn't enjoy him too.

REGER

CCXLII. SERENADE IN G MAJOR, FOR ORCHESTRA, OP. 95

1 *Allegro moderato.* 2 *Vivace a Burlesca.* 3 *Andante semplice.* 4 *Allegro con spirito.*

The Orchestral Serenade, opus 95, ought to be the work by which the public has learnt to enjoy Reger. Yet it seems to have fallen into neglect. There is no reason why the most esoteric disciple of Reger should wish it to be neglected, for it is intensely characteristic of him and in no way superficial or misrepresentative of his message to the world. Yet it has a surface beauty so extraordinary and so directly convincing, that it was one of the very few modern works which Joachim in the last years of his life was able to enjoy. Any fool could, and many fools did, gibe at Joachim's inability in old age to enjoy new music. But only wise and unselfish people are capable of the great and constant efforts that Joachim made to appreciate new works up to the end of his life, and, to those who knew him well enough to see how great these efforts were, it was a touching and historic moment when he introduced this Serenade to the students of the Hochschule at Berlin, as a work unquestionably of the highest importance, though representing tendencies which he did not profess to follow. It was produced almost immediately after Max Reger's most notorious work, his Sinfonietta, a work which begins as naïvely as that famous line, 'Who wills may hear Sordello's story told', and continues as much to the bewilderment of every one whose will has failed to carry him through that story. Of the first performance of the Sinfonietta it is recorded that the eminent and witty conductor Siegfried Ochs, on leaving the concert-room, gave a pat on the back to the notorious composer of *Ein Heldenleben* and the *Sinfonia Domestica*, saying: 'H'm, h'm, I come back to my dear old Strauss.' The Sinfonietta is not markedly different from Reger's other works, except in the very dangerous defect that its orchestration, if taken in strict accordance with the over-numerous directions of the composer, is very thick and extremely shrill. In spite of its already being his 90th opus, it shows the inexperience of a scholar who has developed rule-of-thumb procedures with an intensity that entirely defeats their object; the typical work, in fact, of a pupil of Hugo Riemann, whose editions of the musical classics are so instructive that I find I need a quarter of an hour to practise the subject of a two-part fugue of Bach in accordance with the instructions, and that the simultaneous playing of the two voices when the answer arrives is definitely beyond my capacity. But Reger was an artist who learnt quickly from experience and whose talent for composition was irrepressible, even beneath the weight of the Riemannian steam-roller. Between opus 90 and opus 95, that is to say between the Sinfonietta and this serenade, Reger somehow contrived to clear up his orchestration so far that even a rough first rehearsal of the Serenade produces an astonishingly beautiful texture. And a naïve listener may for some time be satisfied to leave it at that. It is an utter mistake to regard Reger as continuing either the tradition of Brahms or any other classical tradition.

The enormous apparent complexity of his music is merely a widely diffused complexity of texture. Even as such it has its psychologically well-timed changes and moments of relief. You cannot improvise on a keyboard in such a texture, but Reger could and did improvise on paper.

The fact that a large proportion of his works is in sonata form is frankly and literally neither here nor there, at all events in the classical sense of sonata style. The sonata style will never be understood by people who do not realize that it is primarily and intensely dramatic. Mozart is the one triumphant exception to the rule that the writers of absolute music are not writers for the stage; and the reason for this exception is partly that Mozart's talent was universal, but also that that talent came into the world at exactly the right moment for simultaneously dramatizing the sonata style and giving perfect musical form to the treatment of situations on the stage. It is difficult to say what Reger would have done with an opera. His temperament goes with an abhorrence of staginess which would exclude that quality from the stage itself if it could. What is quite certain is that his mastery of the external forms of classical music was completely irrelevant to music drama. But my own opinion is that it was equally irrelevant to his own music, and that it did it neither good nor harm. He set up the proportions of sonata forms *a priori* and filled them out with his music.

One of the greatest masters of the art of extemporizing, living here in Edinburgh, was overheard by me, after the conclusion of one of his unrecorded symphonic poems, to answer an indiscreet question of an admirer: 'No, my fugue wouldn't bear analysis.' But it would very well have borne hearing again, if one could recapture it; and I am not much interested in the kind of analysis that such music will not bear. Reger's music will, no doubt, bear that kind of analysis, as well as the analysis that I believe in. His classical forms are according to the definitions in Riemann's dictionary. But to identify them as such will not help the listener. My own belief is that it does not help with classical music; for I find that, if I have to analyse a great classic with any efficiency, I must go from phrase to phrase as if there was no *a priori* definable form at all. I call the result a classical form when this process of detailed analysis convinces me that the form is the inevitable result of the material, and that the question which came first is a merely practical matter of no aesthetic importance. In the case of highly dramatic works, close attention may be needed for minute details which the further course of the work may show to be as enormous in their consequences as the depth into which the parsley sank into the butter on a hot day in one of Sherlock Holmes's

unrecorded cases. When such a story is well told, these fatal details
are put clearly enough in the first instance for an attentive memory
to recognize their importance without undue length of recapitulation when the time comes for explanations. Now far be it from me
to insinuate that the listener who misses any of Reger's fine detail
has not missed something of importance. But I can assure him
that what he will miss will be such matters of proportion as are
never appreciated until you have known your music by heart for
years, and that, for all the extraordinary elaboration of Reger's
scores, that composer is as inveterate an extemporizer as Handel;
though, unlike Handel, his texture is never either simple or
thin, and every scrap of his extemporization has been most meticulously written down. His adherence to the externals of sonata
form is, in this serenade as in all his chamber-music, so strict
that the old-fashioned terminology will do for every stage of the
work.

The main themes of the first movement of this serenade are so
attractive and so nearly normal in their phrasing that the first
impression of that movement ought to suffice to carry the listener
through the whole of the rest, however unfamiliar Reger's style
may be to him. It is not often that Reger gives his melodies so much
time to explain themselves as is the case with Exx. 1 and 3. It is
part of his view of musical history that modern progress has made
the building of square-cut melodies an anachronism; and the
avoidance of squareness is a restriction which Reger has con-
sciously laid upon his methods of extemporizing. You may take
it, therefore, that the quotations I have thought necessary to give,
though they are far from representing every theme in his Serenade,
do as a matter of fact represent all there is of each theme. How
far Reger is a composer of large paragraphs I cannot show in a
short analysis. I have never yet found him at a loss. His sentences
are as infallible as Gladstone's, who is said never to have required
correction in Hansard, though he could do without a full stop
for pages together.

The listener who is not familiar with Reger's style will, then,
need reassurance on these points: first, that his attention may be
safely concentrated on what is in fact the rule of safety for all
music—listen from one moment to the next and, if the texture is
rich, enjoy it as such. Secondly, do not be bewildered by Reger's
constant changes of key. This hardly applies to the present work,
though opening themes in G major do not usually make their
first modulation to F sharp major. If the poet tells you that 'he
thought that he saw a rattlesnake which questioned him in Greek,
And when he looked again it was the middle of next week', you
had better listen for the continuation in a calmly receptive mood

before you try to summarize the poet's philosophy. He may be intending to give simple pleasure without any purpose of inculcating philosophy. As a matter of fact, the modulations in this Serenade are not very confusing, and its only non-classical feature of tonality is the key of the slow movement, A major, which Brahms would never have dreamt of choosing as an element in a work in G.

The scoring of the Serenade divides the string band into two complete groups, one muted and the other unmuted. In a footnote the composer requests that the unmuted orchestra be placed as far as possible to the conductor's left and the muted orchestra to his right. I came to my first rehearsal of the work full of zeal to carry out this direction, which I found placed beyond all human ingenuity by the fact that each muted part was printed on the same pages as the corresponding unmuted part in order that both might be played by the players at one desk. It seems that before the parts were printed Reger had already found that the muted band was quite enough handicapped by its mutes without the additional disadvantage of sitting in the position of second violins with instruments turned away from the audience. In his next important work, opus 100, Variations on a Theme by Adam Hiller, he uses this division of the orchestra in passages here and there. Obviously there is no time in such a case to play a game of musical chairs while the orchestra rearranges itself, and Reger evidently found that the antiphonal effect of a change of position was not worth the trouble.

The listener will find already in the course of Ex. 1 that the change of colour with the third bar is an experience unlike anything in earlier music and quite thrilling enough to set the standard for his enjoyment of the whole work. In spite of an apparent inability to resist the temptation to indulge in such luxuries as harp-harmonics on every convenient occasion, Reger's profound rhetorical instinct always keeps his music on the alert. You will find no difficulty in following it if you will only abandon your mind to it and refuse to be misled by its outward conformity to the rules of sonata music. I do not quote anything like the complete stock of Reger's themes, and I have very little curiosity as to how far the themes which I do quote may be discovered to be derived from each other. 'Let go your hands and your feet and you'll come down by yourself,' as the steward of the Clyde steamer said to the testy passenger who asked how he was to negotiate the saloon stairs.

Here are three themes from the first movement; the main theme, which haunts not only the listener's memory, but the last bars of each of the other movements—

a subsidiary theme—

and the chief theme of the second group—

The dramatic end of the exposition shows the quintessence of Reger's rhetoric.

The development begins with a dramatic and impressive augmentation of the figures of Ex. 1. Though its course comprises a vigorous fugue on derivative themes it is not inordinately long. The return is effected quietly but dramatically after Reger has combined Exx. 1 and 3 simultaneously. At the beginning of the recapitulation a new figure—

is combined with Ex. 1. Its whimsical purpose will appear later. When the recapitulation has reached Ex. 4 a typical short Reger coda follows, consisting of a ritardando that, with a plunge into

the warm dark key of B flat, loses the original tempo altogether
and re-establishes the home tonic in an ever-slackening adagio.
Such an obliteration of tempo is quite outside all precedent in
recorded classical art-forms, but is very familiar to the church
organist, who has to continue his extemporization until the clergy
and choir are ready to begin the service. As successor to a certain
J. S. Bach in the Cantorship of St. Thomas at Leipzig, Reger is
familiar with all the devices of church organists; and any musician
who is so snobbish as to object to such devices *a priori*, deserves
the snub of the grim old lady in the omnibus who said to the
young person who was afraid of being taken for a shop-girl: 'I
hope, my dear, that you will never be taken for anything less respectable.' These organist's 'trailers' of Reger's are among the
most beautiful things in the music of the early twentieth century.

The tiny little scherzo has no trio, though it has more themes
than the contrasted couple which I quote.

Ex. 5.

Ex. 6.

It soon surprises us by a sudden loss of momentum, and ends by
slackening to an adagio close in which Ex. 1 appears as a penultimate flat supertonic.

The slow movement, in the entirely unorthodox key of A major,
is a rondo, inasmuch as its main theme—

Ex. 7.

though not built into any too square-cut a melody for Reger's
taste, alternates with two distinct episodes, recurring several times
and giving a full sonata-like recapitulation of the first episode in
the tonic. A transition-theme—

Ex. 8.

leads to the first episode, which is in the dominant. I give the
whole theme of the episode, to show that Reger is by no means
afraid of giving a long melody to the first violins without breaking

it up. Figure *x*, from the first movement, will surprise the attentive listener by appearing here among the accessory counterpoints.

Ex. 9.

The second episode introduces a new theme in a warm dark key
(F major, here nearly equivalent to, but relatively darker than the
B flat at the end of the first movement)—

Ex. 10.

This leads to considerable development of the previous material.
In due time the main theme (Ex. 7) returns with very gorgeous
scoring and is followed by a recapitulation, full but free, of the
transition and first episode in the tonic. Slow as is the tempo, the
coda again gives us an organist's ritardando, and the enormous
last bar contains two distinct allusions to Ex. 1.

The finale is spirited and energetic, with a typical crowd of
Reger themes all as pretty as the stories in the dictionary and all
as 'unco short'.

I select, with no very strong case for preference, two from the
first group in the tonic—

Ex. 11.

and a theme leading to the second group—

Ex. 13.

and the main theme of the second group—

Ex. 14.

The movement is in full sonata form. The course of the development is deflected by an episode in double fugue which obviously
owes one of its figures to the semiquavers in Ex. 12—

Ex. 15.

After a triumphant return and full recapitulation the coda turns
into a mood of Prospero-like reflection and solemn peace, recalling
and developing the figures of Ex. 1 in a slow climax of euphony
that gloriously crowns the work. Figure *x* also gives its blessing
to the coda.

MAHLER

CCXLIII. SYMPHONY IN G MAJOR, NO. 4

1 *Bedächtig.* (*Moderato.*) 2 *In gemächlicher Bewegung. Ohne Hast.* (*At a
deliberate pace; unhurried.*) 3 *Ruhevoll.* (*Calm.*) 4 *Sehr behaglich.* (*Very
comfortably.*)

Mahler was born in 1860, and died in 1911. He earned his reputation as one of the world's greatest conductors. As a composer he
fascinated a few musicians, but infuriated almost all the rest.
The fury that he aroused was not partisan like that aroused by the
compositions of Liszt. Even at the present day people who dislike
Liszt are repelled, as Ruskin would have been repelled, by qualities
to which they impute a sinister ethical significance. This is not
altogether to Liszt's disadvantage. People who believe in the devil
are either too much horrified by their belief to tolerate the slightest
mention of him, or they find a naughty thrill in playing with their
superstition. On the whole, a belief in the devil is a superstition
which is likely to survive, and even to flourish when all other
capacity for belief is exhausted. It is so very easy to live up to.

And it supplies ready-made every conceivable gradation of contrast, and can give to the most facile pathos the apparent strength
of sardonic humour. In the time of Ruskin and Clara Schumann
it was impossible not to be angry when the devil interfered in
aesthetic questions, as he always did.

The opposition to Mahler is angrier, less serious, and more
damaging. In Holland Mahler has for the last fifteen years or so
been as nearly deified as any composer in history. This is odd,
because there is perhaps no country in which musical criticism is
more *blasé* towards older music. A great artist not long ago ventured to play in Holland Joachim's Hungarian Concerto, which I
personally regard as a work not only of immense historical importance, but a monumental accumulation of beautiful musical thoughts
second only to the greatest classics, and of a quality which none
of the greatest masters could afford to despise. The most eminent
Dutch critics were agreed in wondering that such stuff had ever
been published at all. No great insight is needed to discover a
certain stiffness in Joachim's style as a composer. And as for its
relation to earlier classical music, no listener need be a listener at
all to discover its derivation. We have been told all about that.
Let us hope that the vogue of Mahler in Holland is already a sign
that anti-classical snobbery is becoming out of fashion. For the
infuriating quality of Mahler's music is particularly antiseptic
against snobs, though perhaps it cannot prevent the rise of Mahlerite snobs. There is no class of composer, diabolist or purist,
for whom a first impression of Mahler will not cause pangs of
jealousy. Mahler is no Shakespeare, and few, if any of us, are
Coleridges; but we could all write like that 'if we had the mind'.
He has no inhibitions. The experienced composer, academic,
revolutionary, self-centred in Delian or Debussian circles ever
narrowing, or eclectic in an expanding Straussian universe, encounters the style and achievements of Mahler with something of
the horror which we are told that Dr. 'Froyd' evinced when the
blonde lady revealed to him that she had neither dreams nor
inhibitions, and that she never did not do anything 'vialent' that
she wanted to do, though 'the bullet only went into Mr. Jenning's
lung and came out again'.

My own belief is that a vogue for Mahler has already been of
great benefit to musical culture all over the world, and will continue to be useful for a longer time than I can estimate. There is
a fundamental inaccuracy in saying that an artist has too much
facility, unless we make it quite clear that we mean by 'facility' the
condition in which the artist's thoughts have no chance of maturing.
A tree that needs pruning may be said to have too much facility in
producing leaves, but its trouble is that until it is pruned it has very

little facility for producing fruit. The stream which spreads itself into an unwholesome marsh instead of developing into a mighty river is not suffering from too much facility or too much water. It has simply not been helped by nature or art to dig a proper channel in which its waters can accumulate.

In the last resort, every artist needs all the facility he can get. What we composers find so disconcerting about Mahler is that every aspect of his work shows all the advantages of an unchecked facility and none of the disadvantages. It has us beaten at every point, and leaves us no resource but to sit upright in our dignity as men of taste and say, 'This will never do.' We cannot fall back upon the device of classifying Mahler as one of the conductor-composers who have drifted into composition through the urge to display their vast memories as experienced conductors. Mahler was only twenty when he produced his first important work, *Das Klagende Lied.* We cannot say that his music is reminiscent, for our chief objection to it is that no other composer has had the effrontery to proceed further with the ideas that give Mahler his simple pleasures. The very first note of his First Symphony is a sustained A eight octaves deep. I do not suppose that I was the only eleven-year-old child to whom it occurred to strike, with the aid of two other children, all the eight A's on the pianoforte. Weber thought Beethoven ripe for the madhouse when Beethoven in the coda of the first movement of his Seventh Symphony held a sustained E five octaves deep. But that was in a passage with a long history of highly organized development behind it; and it is curious that Weber did not rather select the five-octave B flat at the very beginning of Beethoven's Fourth Symphony, though he had already cited that introduction with scorn as an instance of the bluff of spreading a dozen notes over a quarter of an hour.

These illustrations will give the devout Mahlerite his cue for claiming that history is repeating itself by displaying exactly the same opposition to Mahler as was shown to Beethoven in his day. We need not trouble to discuss the inference that Mahler is another Beethoven; and, though history repeats itself, its variations are extremely difficult to analyse. But we can say with certainty that Mahler's example has set modern composers free from inhibitions which were for the most part harmful and snobbish. He has been a greater liberator in this way than Richard Strauss, for Strauss indulges his vein of naïve melody under the pretext of caricature. Till Eulenspiegel and Don Quixote are his heroes. The element of caricature is present in Mahler, but he is terrified lest it should be suspected where he is as unconscious of it as Dickens in his most conscientiously pathetic passages. Nothing can lend itself more to caricature than the grotesque folk-pastoral poem from *Des*

Knaben Wunderhorn, but Mahler's direction to the singer is: 'The voice with an expression of childlike cheerfulness without the slightest suspicion of parody.' In the twentieth century it is impossible for an artist to indulge himself with simple forms and simple melodies without feeling conscious of the dangers of affectation or caricature. Mahler is so enormously rich in every technical resource that, as Röntgen used to say, one cannot trust his simplicity. This pastoral style is *à la campagne*, and Marie Antoinette could be *à la campagne* at the Trianons.

On the other hand, the most devout Mahlerite will hardly claim that the master's style is aristocratic, either by nature or by affectation. On the whole, we composers and men of taste will be well advised to abandon our opposition, for if we persist in it there is no point on which we can clear ourselves from the suspicion of being jealous. Mahler did not care two hoots for popularity. He was extremely exacting as a conductor, and was sometimes in bodily peril from the anger roused by his ruthless efforts in raising the standard of the Vienna Opera House to its supreme height. In point of style he might be called a musical Dickens born out of season. In every technical direction—form, counterpoint, and instrumentation—his musical facility is so enormous that we cannot compare him to any of the other *monstr'-inform'-ingent'-horrendi* masters that otherwise resemble him, and who become objects of fanatical worship at the expense of the more orthodox classics. And so the opposition to Mahler deprives him even of the martyr's crown. We do not wish it generally known, but we would all like to write like Mahler if we dared; and we all think that we could. The martyr whom he most nearly resembles is Bruckner, but Mahler is anything but helpless, and rouses none of the sympathy of a naïve artist struggling for self-expression. Far from it. We find his facility deadly. His Third Symphony is a musical phantasmagoria in which all the elements that have ever been put into a symphony before are conglomerated with all the musical equivalents of a picaresque novel and a Christmas pantomime. It was intelligently anticipated by Aristophanes in a word beginning *lepado-temacho . . .* and filling six or seven lines in Liddell and Scott's Lexicon. On internal evidence it was written during a holiday at Llanfairpwllgwyngyllgogerychwyrndrobwll-llantysiliogogogoch. Yet the history of this Third Symphony shows that Mahler could exercise artistic restraint; for he so compressed its plan that he extruded one of its items, which he preserved for a more conspicuous existence as the finale of his Fourth Symphony.

The musical culture of Great Britain will probably be the better for the rise of a vogue for Bruckner and Mahler; and perhaps

Mahler will do us more good than Bruckner, because his mastery will discourage the cult of amateurishness, which keeps us contented with ignorance and ready to believe that ineptitude is noble in itself; and the good taste which is ready to take offence at Mahler's sentimentality will be all the better for being shocked. It will find itself compelled to recognize that the difference between good and bad is not a matter of fashion; though, with all respect to Horace, it can never cease to be a matter of dispute. For my own part, I flatly refuse to class Mahler with either Liszt or Meyerbeer. Liszt is for me a composer whose art has a definite taint which ruins my enjoyment of much that would otherwise fascinate me. Meyerbeer is a very clever, and sometimes very inventive, composer who is such a thorough humbug that I cannot regard him as a real person at all, and cannot be bothered to argue with people who can. There will be reservations with all such matters; and I am entirely in agreement with Wagner, who had the courage to scandalize all his friends by praising in the highest terms the duet at the end of the fourth act of *Les Huguenots*; but one decent moment will not make Meyerbeer into a good artist, and all the bad taste of Dickens, Victor Hugo, Byron, and Berlioz will not make Mahler a bad composer.

Mahler's Fourth Symphony is pastoral throughout. The orchestra pretends to be small, inasmuch as it has no trombones and only four horns. On the other hand, it is very expensive in extra wood-wind, and denies itself nothing in what is known as the 'kitchen department', such as sleighbells and gongs. The first movement begins with farm-yard noises—

Ex. 1.

on a B minor chord, through which the violins swing into G major with the gallantry of a rustic who has been to town.

Ex. 2.

I quote scarcely half the large number of themes that Mahler pours out and adorns with instrumentation and counterpoint of infallible mastery and clearness. The counterstatement of Ex. 2

is in free canon, combined in the third bar with a casual counter-point which afterwards becomes an important theme.

Ex. 2 a.

Another pair of yokels in double counterpoint—

Ex. 3.

leads to the dominant, upon which, with the abruptness of Mozart's most perfunctory style, the 'second subject' radiates expression from every pore of its infant complexion.

Ex. 4.

&c.

But under this burlesque simplicity the discerning composer may espy the cloven hoof, indicated by dropped and added beats which betray that Mahler's phrase-rhythms are as supple and subtle as his scoring.

I may as well quote one more theme, which brings new elements and leads to the end of the exposition.

Ex. 5.

Its opening figure eventually dies away into the chord of B minor, and the initial farm-yard sounds (Ex. 1) are resumed, leading back to Ex. 2.

The movement now proceeds to shape itself more or less like a rondo, instead of going into a development section. Ex. 2 (a) is expanded into a peaceful tonic-and-dominant die-away, coming to a long-drawn full-close. Then the farm-yard sounds are resumed, and something like a development arises. It develops what it likes, and settles where it likes. It soon makes up its mind that A major is a proper key in which the three repeated notes of Ex. 4 may become a long-drawn 'Cheer, boys, cheer' over ruminations of the figure of Ex. 2 (a). For twenty-three bars this complex, or simplex, refuses to be dislodged from A as its bass-note.

It then strides casually into the middle of next week, which you may call E flat minor if you like; and the other figures of the exposition enter into discussion with each other, modulating rapidly, and sometimes settling to episodic sections in this or that key, always with plenty of variety and quite clear sequence. At last a tremendous climax is reached in C major, with triumphant shouts of the upper theme of Ex. 3. The decline from this leads to the return of the main theme (Ex. 2), but, very cunningly, not to its opening, but to its third bar; as if the theme, after having travelled round the world, were to walk in to breakfast unannounced, remarking, 'As I was saying . . .' It drifts into a recapitulation which is disguised by the fact that much of the matter is now given to the bass with new counterpoint above. The transition theme (Ex. 3) enters in the bass with something of the excitement of the C major climax of the development, and Mahler puts as a mark of expression the word *wild* (ferocious). The 'Cheer-boys-cheer' simplex (Ex. 4) is given with grandiose full tone, which subsides only at the cadence group (Ex. 5). When this has died away the farm-yard sounds are resumed, and the unquoted sequels of Ex. 2 are worked up into a full-sized coda, which eventually settles to a passage of sustained calm developed from Ex. 2 (*a*) and dying away into a very slow allusion to Ex. 2, which quickly hastens its pace and ends the movement in high spirits with a derivative of both members of Ex. 3 compressed like one of Humpty-Dumpty's portmanteau words.

The enemy dare not blaspheme at the themes of the first movement, for to question their originality and distinction is to expose oneself to the charge of not seeing a joke. The themes of the scherzo will hardly give the enemy occasion to blaspheme, whether he likes them or not, for they are unquestionably original; and, if their spice has a smell of garlic, this is at all events a rural smell. The key of the movement is C minor, but it arises from an introduction in an outlying region.

Ex. 6.

A solo violin enters aggressively (*sehr zufahrend*), and wrenches the harmony round to C minor with the following sour theme—

Ex. 7.

You will notice that the tone of the instrument is not exactly that
of a Stradivarius played by Joachim. Mahler's direction is *wie ein
Fiedel,* which may be rendered 'like a kit', or 'fiddle' if you like;
and the long-suffering player has to play upon a violin that has
endured the indignity of being tuned a tone higher.

The movement trips its leisurely way through a free rondo form
to which the episodes might give the impression of a scherzo with
two trios—

Ex. 8.

but for the fact that they return at once to the main theme before
they round themselves off. The form assumes a more important
aspect after the second return of the main theme, for then the
material of both trios is elaborated in a spacious development,
which goes through many keys before finally settling down in C
major in a coda in which all the figures of scherzo and trios are
discussed in dialogue.

The third movement is in a kind of variation form to which the
nearest parallel may be found in the middle movement of Sibelius's
Fifth Symphony. The theme is no fixture, either as bass, melody
or scheme of harmonies. Its constant element is a type of bass, the
course of which follows the convenience of the moment; and over
this bass long-drawn melodies and counterpoints ruminate at
leisure.

Ex. 10.

Thus it is impossible to limit the theme or to count the variations.
After sixty bars Mahler makes a definite change of key to E minor,
where, in a much slower tempo, an oboe sings a dirge over a
version of the bass figure which is diminished from crotchets to
quavers. The dirge, taken up by other instruments, develops
with great passion, and a return is gradually made to the home
tonic. The effect of a ritardando followed by a change to a tempo
twice as fast makes it impossible to distinguish the diminished

version from the original version of the bass. In a footnote,
Mahler now admits that he is writing a variation. The new counterpoints are richer, and the pace accelerates. Like the first variation-
group, this one dies away, and the dirge complex is resumed,
starting in G minor and passing soon into the remote key of C sharp
minor. After an impassioned climax in this key, it subsides into
a new group of variations passing one into another with absolutely
abrupt changes of tempo: first andante 3/4 time, then allegretto
3/8, and then in E major allegro 2/4, quickening to allegro
molto and suddenly falling back to andante. Upon this there is
a long-drawn coda, which is dying away peacefully in G major
when suddenly there is a tremendous burst of glory in E major,
a key for which the E minor of the dirge has not prepared us. The
glory dies away in a haze of light, passing back into G major and
expiring very slowly on its dominant.

The discerning listener may perhaps have heard a figure for
four horns before the expiry of the outburst in E major which
surprised us so at the end of the slow movement. I have not
quoted this figure, because Mahler has taken more trouble to bring
out another shrill motive in the trumpets. But from this figure
arise the first notes of the soprano song with which the symphony
ends.

Ex. 11.

Wie ge-nies - sen die himm - e - - - - li - schen Freu - den

The words are a poem from the famous anthology of folk poetry,
Des Knaben Wunderhorn. The orchestra supplies preludes and
interludes and an extremely delicate and highly coloured accompaniment. I forbear to transcribe or translate the poem word by
word. No reasonable person will be shocked at its innocent pro-
fanity; but until we have all learned to accept Mahler as a classic,
we had better not expose him to the blasphemy of the enemy who
would cast doubts upon the composer's reverence for sacred
subjects. Lewis Carroll, in his *alter ego* as the Rev. C. L. Dodgson,
was severe in his condemnation of those who quoted the innocent
profanities of children and then pleaded the innocence of the child
as if it was their own innocence. He did not consider the possibility
that one might quote innocent blasphemies with something like
reverence for the innocence. Certainly it is difficult to imagine that
anybody would quote them, as Dodgson implied, for the jejune
purpose of blaspheming.

I have already remarked on Mahler's emphatic forbidding of
any touch of parody in the performance of this finale. The poem

describes the pleasures of a simple soul in Heaven, far from the strife of the world, which exists only in order that *Weltgetümmel* may rhyme with *Himmel*, as it does in Bach's most solemn cantatas. We live an angelic life and dance and skip while St. Peter in Heaven looks on.

Ex. 12.

Sankt Pe - ter im   Him - mel sieht   zu l

The next stanza brings back and develops the farm-yard sounds of the first movement. A certain savagery in the tone is accounted for by the fact that Herod is the accepted Family Butcher in this unorthodox heaven, and that St. John and St. Luke allow him a free hand. St. Luke kills his ox, the wine of the heavenly cellars costs nothing, and the angels bake the bread.

The third stanza describes the heavenly vegetable gardens, with gardeners who, contrary to the severe baronial Scottish tradition, will let you have everything. Game of all sorts runs towards you, and all manner of fish swim into St. Peter's net.

With one more short farm-yard interlude from Ex. 1, the music subsides into E major, thus accounting for the outburst in that key at the end of the slow movement. Mahler's harmony is the most diatonic that has been heard since classical times, though it has no inhibitions whatever. His classical keys and his other ancient and modern modes are always perfectly clear; but he does not feel any obligation to end a symphony or a movement in the key in which it began, and so his Fourth Symphony, after having been as firmly centred round G major as any symphony of Haydn, calmly subsides into E major for the last stanza of its final song, which describes the music of Heaven, with St. Ursula smiling upon her eleven thousand virgin dancers, and St. Cecilia and all her relations as the most excellent of court musicians.

After all, we have the authority of Dante in more than one of the sublimest passages of the *Paradiso* for supposing that, though Heaven is not confined to what any mortal can understand, it includes all that we can understand. Bruckner understood considerably less of most things than Mahler. He would probably have been horrified at the notion of setting this poem. I, for my part, would be horrified at the idea of Meyerbeer setting it. Mahler I suspect of having wept as copiously over it as Dickens over Little Nell or Macaulay over the end of the *Iliad*. Such a temper has its dangers for judges and dictators; but it is much more useful in the present state of music than tastes that are too refined for Beethoven, and it is positively antiseptic against many types of morbid art. For Mahler himself the safeguard lies in his enormous technique; and for students of all kinds of musical technique Mahler will be none the less use to them if they are shocked by him.

ELGAR

CCXLIV. CONCERT OVERTURE, 'IN THE SOUTH' (ALASSIO), OP. 50

I have not been to Alassio, and so I cannot talk of Elgar's special sources of inspiration for this brilliant and sunshiny overture. I only hope that, if I ever do go there, I may not find myself in the position of the old lady who said to Turner that she could not see in sunsets anything like his pictorial representations of them; to which, of course, he replied, 'Don't you wish you could?' If she could, she would not have been able to find words for them; and if ever I can see at places like Alassio what Elgar saw as he saw it, I would much rather write a concert overture about it than an analytical programme.

There is still a suspicion of faintness in praising a work for its orchestration, though the time has perhaps passed since nobility was thought to be inherent in clumsy scoring; but, so long as tastes differ as to a composer's style, there is something to be said for calling the listener's attention to a merit which every competent judge must admit to be supreme, not only in its artistic results, but in its practical efficiency. I shall not easily forget my impression when, on first attacking this overture with considerable fear and expectation of its being as difficult as it is brilliant, I found that it simply carried the orchestra away with it and seemed to play itself at the first rehearsal. On inquiry, I found that one single member of the orchestra was not reading it at sight. This exception, of course, accounted for the whole phenomenon, and I am far from claiming that the rehearsal was such as I should willingly accept in lieu of a performance. But I and my students have never had a more impressive demonstration of the enormous efficiency of Elgar's scoring. In brilliance the nearest approach to it in other modern music is the scoring of Richard Strauss; and Elgar and Strauss have in common a panache which is popularly expressed in both the title and the substance of Elgar's *Pomp and Circumstance* Marches, and mystically expressed in the best parts of Strauss's *Heldenleben*. But the scores of Strauss bristle with technical abnormalities, and he drives through his musical traffic like a road-hog, with a mastery that has merely overawed the police without reforming the rules of the road. Some think that even *Ein Heldenleben* is now wearing too thin to reward the labour of thirty rehearsals for the purpose of securing accuracy where the composer merely intends effrontery.

To the Straussian panache Elgar adds the enormous sonority and cogency of a style which is meticulously pure. This is a matter of fact, and not of taste. Perhaps the word 'meticulous' may be misleading, and 'classical' might be a better epithet. But I think 'meticulous' is right. Whether you are carried away by Elgar's style or whether you dislike it, there is no doubt that it is not the style of a man who is at ease in himself or in Zion. Neither in poetry nor in music is the atmosphere of *The Dream of Gerontius* that of a muscular Christian after Charles Kingsley's heart; and those for whom Kipling's sixth-form imperialism obliterates his art will not like *Pomp and Circumstance*. But I should be surprised if the most nervous of reasonable music-lovers could not enjoy *In the South*. When it appeared in 1904, any approach to mastery of instrumental form on the part of a British composer was still considered dangerous. I cannot remember whether *In the South* had a better reception than the *Cockaigne* Overture; but it is both a larger and a simpler work, of which the portion normally devoted to developments is occupied by two detachable episodes. When Steinbach conducted it at a concert of English music at Cologne in, I think, 1906, I was surprised to find that he thought it patchy. That impression probably arose from these episodes, but I am sure that it is a superficial impression, perhaps intensified by the comparative orthodoxy and greater concentration of the other works played on that occasion. In itself, *Alassio* is by no means a loose-knit work. It has more unity than the *Enigma* Variations, and far more coherence than Elgar's First Symphony. Classical overtures, especially when they are preludes to operas, do not profess to have the concentrated texture of symphonic movements, and my most beloved overtures of Weber are things of shreds and patches compared to *Alassio*.

Elgar begins with a group of heroic themes swinging along at full speed from the outset.

There are more of these than it is necessary to quote, but Ex. 1 shows itself as a counterpoint to all the others. The initial impetus

is strong enough to survive a solemn climax marked by Elgar's favourite direction, *Nobilmente*.

After an apparently casual incident in the decline—

a pair of gentler themes appears in C minor—

and leads to a quiet second group, passionately lyrical, in duple time and the extremely unorthodox key of F major.

Ex. 7.

Ex. 8.

Even in the tranquillity of Ex. 8, Ex. 1 intrudes as a counterpoint. Soon Exx. 5 and 6 bring about a gradual revival of energy and carry us into the current of a vigorous development. But this does not last long before we are confronted with a terrifically impressive structure.

Ex. 9.

Ex. 10.

I shall be highly pleased with myself if any Roman bridge or
viaduct, at Alassio or elsewhere, can make an impression on me
that is not mainly dominated by my knowledge of this magnificent
passage with its superbly proportioned repetitions, climax, and
diminuendo. People differ greatly in the extent to which sounds
suggest visual impressions. With me this happens very rarely, but
then very intensely; and Ex. 10 gives me the strongest suggestion
of a horizontal line of roadway immensely high up, with the piers
descending from it into greater and greater depths along a precipi-
tous hill-side.

After the vision has become distant, the progress of development
is resumed with a new bustling theme.

Ex. 11.

Eventually Ex. 1 intervenes, and there is another glimpse of the
bridge or viaduct before Ex. 11 is resumed. The incident quoted
in Ex. 4 becomes important in an impressive diminuendo, typical
of Elgar's most mystic style; and eventually we have what has
become known in a separate arrangement as a piece for small
orchestra, *Canto Popolare* (*In Moonlight*). As a separate piece it is
a very pretty thing, but in its context in this Overture it is as gravely
and romantically beautiful as music can be.

Ex. 12.
Viola solo.

Quiet and slow reminiscences of Ex. 1 intervene contrapuntally, and
there are warnings of a revival of energy in allusions to Exx. 4 and 5.

The *Canto Popolare* dies away, and in the original key and
tempo Ex. 1 returns pianissimo, but with a rapid crescendo which
soon brings us into the full swing of a regular recapitulation of
everything from Exx. 1 to 8: the F major group from 6 to 7 being,
of course, now in the home tonic. From the quiet end of this
recapitulation arises Ex. 3, a fourth lower and in the tenderest
pianissimo. It swells out and leads to fresh developments of the
livelier themes in a noble coda which is one of the best of all Elgar's
perorations, its rhetoric entirely unspoilt by tub-thumping, and
leaving us with a magnificent impression of punctuality in its end.

CCXLV. INTRODUCTION AND ALLEGRO FOR STRINGS
(QUARTET AND ORCHESTRA), OP. 47

Comparisons of this important work with the concerto grosso of
the early eighteenth century are misleading. In its form and texture there is neither the antiquity of Wardour Streete Englisshe
nor that of the genuine furniture that may be bought in that street
by those who know. It is a piece of modern music, modern in the
lasting sense of the term. That is to say, its date, 1905, is no
more identifiable in 1937 than it will be in 2005. The kind of
concerto form which it embodies is in line with Beethoven and
Brahms, and definitely out of line with Handel and Bach. The
sound of the strings, in both solo and tutti, will remind us of the
older masters, simply because the Concerti Grossi of Handel and
his predecessors and the third Brandenburg Concerto of Bach are
the only classical works for string orchestra that we ever hear, with
the solitary exception of Mozart's toy masterpiece, *Eine Kleine
Nachtmusik*. But if it had ever occurred to Beethoven or Brahms
to experiment with the problem of concerto form for an orchestra
of strings alone, they would have produced something with the
essential features of the present work. It is highly probable that,
like Elgar, they would have treated the contrast between string
quartet and string tutti as rather a matter of fine shades than of the
intense dramatic opposition of solo and orchestra that inspired
them when the orchestra was full. Also the fitness of the occasion
for fugue-writing would not have escaped their notice, nor would
they have been slow to take advantage of it.

In the present work, as in others, Elgar's form is his own; and
doubtless Beethoven and Brahms would each have achieved a
different and unique solution of its special problem. A long
classical orchestral ritornello has another function besides that of
giving scope to the full orchestra. It presents the main features
of the movement in an introductory form. This introduction

naturally has a processional character when the ritornello is long; and only something highly dramatic can be justified in curtailing it. Hence nothing could be more appropriate than that, instead of the formal ritornello, the present work should have a grand introduction in which the themes appear at first as fragments in a highly dramatic dialogue between orchestra and quartet; the united forces propounding a sternly majestic question—

to which the quartet adds another in wistful tones—

After the dialogue has made some progress with the discussion the viola is allowed to give full lyric form to a new melody in E flat—

which the quartet and orchestra take up with quiet enthusiasm. Ex. 1 intervenes again dramatically, bringing back the key of G minor. The lyric melody pathetically accepts the decision; but its dying fall, after a long pause, resolves in the cheerful and active daylight with which the allegro now begins.

Nobody could have foreseen what the functions of these themes are now to be. Ex. 2, with its typically Elgaresque quick dactylic figure, becomes the main theme. A new three-bar theme, stated in a lower octave by the quartet and answered by the tutti—

executes a broadly designed transition to the dominant, in which key the second group begins in triumph. The *a-priori* theorist expects it to consist of an enlargement of the lyric melody, Ex. 3. It proves, on the contrary, to consist of a grand tutti on Ex. 1, in terms of the utmost confidence and power, worked out in a brilliant paragraph, the close of which is reached through an allusion to Ex. 4. Suddenly, as the figure of Ex. 1 reverberates above, through and below the last chords, the beginning of the

lyric melody is faintly heard in a tremulous unison of the muted
string quartet—a moment of romantic power worthy to be set by
the Romanza in the *Enigma* Variations. A lively fugue in G minor
has the function of the development-portion of the work. It exercises this function the more efficiently by being completely independent of previous themes. In all genuine concerto styles the
exposition itself is compelled by circumstances to have many
features more typical of development than of exposition; and thus
only by means of episodic matter can the development-portion
maintain a character of its own.

Here is the new fugue-subject—

Ex. 5.

The key-changes of fugues are necessarily drifting rather than
sharply contrasted. In as far as a fugue can be dramatic it is a
debate; and dramatic action will probably stop a debate altogether. Hence Elgar leaves us to discover only when this debate
has reached its climax that we have been at home in the tonic all
the time. (No two works could be less like each other than this
allegro and the finale of Beethoven's Sonata, op. 101, but you will
find exactly the same phenomenon there, as a result of the same
insight into the nature of music.) As the fugue dies away, allusions
to the transition theme (Ex. 4) indicate that the most episodic of
developments can be organically connected with the exposition so
long as there is a B in Both.

A full and regular recapitulation brings symmetry into the
design; but the symmetry extends beyond the allegro and includes
the Introduction; for the lyric melody, Ex. 3, is now neither a far-
off echo nor a gentle strain with a dying fall for the ear of Duke
Orsino, but a solemn triumphal march of full Elgarian pomp.

Throughout the whole work the instrumentation has all Elgar's
subtlety and consummate mastery, shown more obviously by the
limited means here available, though not more perfectly than in
works for full orchestra.

SIBELIUS

CCXLVI. SYMPHONY IN C MAJOR, NO. 7, OP. 105

In spite of the violent objection which every self-respecting musician must feel towards the use of good music as a background to
talking and eating, I confess that I was thrilled when, in its New-
Year's-Eve review of 1933, the British Broadcasting Corporation

used a gramophone record of parts of Sibelius's Seventh Symphony as 'slow music' during the recital of the flight over Mount Everest. Let this sentence do duty for all further efforts to describe in words the austere beauty and rare atmosphere of Sibelius's mature style. Unlike mountain atmospheres, however, that of Sibelius is by no means lacking in oxygen.

It is well that this symphony has met with something like proper appreciation while it is still new. That appreciation has not exaggerated its merits; but it has exaggerated one or two aspects, the report of which may alarm the naïve listener. That versatile if Conservative critic, Mr. Punch, has already remarked that the word 'bleak' has been overworked by the exponents of Sibelius. That word might easily be overworked by admirers of Mount Everest or of the moon. For such things it is a jejune epithet, but we need not trouble to find a better. Only a real poet can afford to tell us that the sky is blue, and he probably will not need to call it azure. If the listener can put up with a good description of the flight over Mount Everest he need not be afraid of the bleakness of Sibelius.

Reports of the length and difficulty of this one-movement symphony are more definitely alarming: it has been described as the longest single and continuous design as yet achieved in absolute music; and experts who have discovered the main theme, as given three times by the first trombone (near the beginning, towards the middle, and at the end), have announced that discovery as the result of a closer familiarity with a complex work. As to its length as a single design, it is not much longer than Leonora No. 3, or the first movement of Schubert's G major Quartet, and not as long as Beethoven's *Grosse Fuge*, which was intended to be the finale of a quartet in six movements, but which makes no allusion to the themes of the other five. As to its difficulty, far be it from me to underrate the technical difficulties of any work for which the rare (and, in this category, unoxygenated) musical-economic atmosphere of Modern Athens gives its orchestral players only six hours' practice a week. Nothing is easy in such conditions; but Sibelius was a very experienced composer many years ago, and this is his opus 105. But the work has a reputation for complexity as well; and this is misleading. Subtlety is quite a different thing, and easily misunderstood; but nobody ever began to understand subtleties by suspecting complexities that do not exist.

In any tolerably competent performance of a typical work of Sibelius, the listener may rest assured that if he finds that an important melodic note has been in existence some time before he was aware of it, the composer has taken special trouble to conceal the beginning of that note. If the listener feels that unformed

fragments of melody loom out of a severely discordant fog of
sound, that is what he is meant to feel. If he cannot tell when or
where the tempo changes, that is because Sibelius has achieved
the power of moving like aircraft, with the wind or against it. An
aeronaut carried with the wind has no sense of movement at all;
but Sibelius's airships are roomy enough for the passengers to dance
if they like: and the landscape, to say nothing of the sky-scape, is
not always too remote for them to judge of the movement of
the ship by external evidences. Sibelius has not only mastered
but made a system of that kind of movement which Wagner
established for music-drama, and which the composers of symphonic poems before Strauss have often failed to achieve and have
not always realized as essential to their problem. Moreover, he
achieves it in absolute music without appealing to any external
programme. He moves in the air and can change his pace without
breaking his movement. The tempi of this Seventh Symphony
range from a genuine adagio to a genuine prestissimo. Time
really moves slowly in the adagio, and the prestissimo arouses the
listener's feeling of muscular movement instead of remaining a
slow affair written in the notation of a quick one. But nobody can
tell how or when the pace, whether muscular or vehicular, has
changed.

An adequate analysis of this noble work would be too subtle to
be readable; and the listener would probably find its points more
evident in the music than in any words. The following five quotations will, I believe, serve the reader's purpose, though there
should be at least ten themes to make a complete list.

The beginning is in darkness, with adumbrations of more than
one future theme. Dawn grows into daylight with a long-drawn
passage beginning with violas and 'cellos and pervading the whole
string-band in a kind of Mixolydian harmony, differing, like all
Sibelius's modal harmony, from Palestrina's only in the boldness
of its dissonances. The winds join towards the climax; and then
the main theme is given out by the first trombone—

Ex. 1.

Fragments of other themes, including figures of the introduction,
follow; and the time quickens gradually, while one of the new
figures gains ascendancy and eventually takes shape as a dance—

Ex. 2.

The pace becomes wild and the modulations far-flung with a new
sequential figure alternating with the second figure of Ex. 2.

Ex. 3.

Yet this muscular energy becomes absorbed quite imperceptibly
into the vast cloud-laden air-currents through and over which
Ex. 1 returns in solemn adagio with C minor harmony. Again the
pace increases; Ex. 3 returns at full speed and leads to new figures,
scudding through the air. (Perhaps you may catch the rhythm of
the trombones—

but the composer marks it pianissimo.) Sunshine emerges upon a
song that would add naïveté to the most innocent shanties of the
human sailors in Wagner's *Flying Dutchman*.

Ex. 4.

This develops, like the earlier themes, with increasing energy and
with several accessories. The climax of its development is cut off
by a momentary allusion to Ex. 3; after which the last phase of the
symphony begins with an accumulation of sequences on the following figures—

Ex. 5.

The presto on the home dominant to which this accumulation
leads proves to be the accompaniment of the final return of Ex. 1
in its proper solemn adagio. With this, and with some of the unquoted introductory figures, the symphony ends in tones of noble
pathos.

CCXLVII. 'TAPIOLA', SYMPHONIC POEM
FOR FULL ORCHESTRA, OP. 112

Tapiola is the god of the northern forests, and the following verses represent the 'programme' of this tone-poem—

> Wide-spread they stand, the Northland's dusky forests,
> Ancient, mysterious, brooding savage dreams;
> Within them dwells the forest's mighty God,
> And wood-sprites in the gloom weave magic secrets.

The music is quintessential Sibelius, and is, perhaps, even more typically than most of his works, describable as a vast and slow crescendo to a climax, after which the descent into silence is short and solemn.

I have attempted on other occasions to write of Sibelius's peculiar methods and art forms, which have always struck me as triumphantly achieving what Bruckner might have achieved in a purely instrumental music on the Wagnerian time-scale, if only he had not encumbered himself with misconceived survivals of sonata form. Sibelius's emancipation from such things is complete, and he is no less independent of the sense of duty which forces the construction of brand-new systems of harmony upon ninety-nine out of a hundred of the composers whose names strike terror into the hearts of simple souls who 'do not like this modern music'. There is plenty of unorthodoxy in Sibelius's harmony, and it has many strange modes, most of them ruthlessly diatonic. But there is no concession to fashion.

Tapiola is a god who pervades a mighty forest; and a detailed analysis of his music will make it impossible for us to see the wood for trees. On the other hand, there is such a thing as having so nobly generalized an idea of the wood as not to be able to know a tree when you see it. Music, after all, must be heard from one moment to the next; and, while there is a strong family resemblance between Sibelius's many short themes which reiterate themselves in emotional outbursts, the listener may find some help in a series of quotations showing roughly how one thing leads to another. The ingenious analysis of the connexion between one theme and another, either by transformation or by figures common to both, is quite beside the mark. More illumination might be obtained by a description of the orchestration, but this again is of use mainly for students who wish to know how to orchestrate, and for conductors who have to realize the composer's intentions. For the listener, a much shorter way to appreciate Sibelius's orchestration is to listen to it. This is particularly easy in *Tapiola*, inasmuch as the orchestral colours not only do not change rapidly, but often show their changes against a background of extraordinary

tone-colour which persists for an amazingly long time, as in the case
of the vast passage which contains Exx. 2, 3, and 4. Here, then, is
an incomplete, but fairly representative, series of the themes, or
phases of themes, which will meet the listener as he wanders
through this dark forest with due reverence for its presiding deity.

With Ex. 5, a lighter tone seems to indicate the 'wood-sprites in
the gloom weaving magic secrets'.

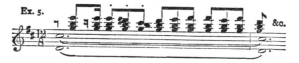

A darker theme emerges in Sibelius's characteristic way at an
unexpected rhythmic point in a long note.

In the course of an ominous crescendo it becomes associated
with another new figure.

Ex. 7.

The crescendo does not fulfil its threat, but passes again into darkness and mystery. Mysterious bright light then appears, with pathetic harmony, high above the gloom.

Ex. 8.

After some time, this unexpectedly gives rise to a formidable crescendo—

Ex. 9.

and a great storm ensues, in which several new figures are heard which I need not quote. The last theme which I shall quote arises from the storm—

Ex. 10.

and soon afterwards the tone-poem takes shape as a purely musical form by means of a definite recapitulation of the group of themes comprised between Exx. 2 and 3 with their strange background.

At last a hurricane rises, which bends the tree-tops and threatens the giants of the forest. The last themes that are heard are a combination of Exx. 8 and 7. The tone-poem then closes with an Amen of slow, bright, major chords, which I give, to save space, in their ancient values of dotted breves and longs.

Ex. 11.

HAVERGAL BRIAN

CCXLVIII. FANTASTIC VARIATIONS ON AN OLD RHYME

I hope that performances of such works as this may draw attention to a composer who has achieved things on a vast scale which may have to wait as long for recognition as usual. This composer will achieve more; but even for the recognition of his smaller works he is being made to wait longer than is good for any composer; and far longer than is good for any country whose musical reputation is worth praying for.

The humour of these Fantastic Variations is dangerously evident. The composer has since written a fantastic opera to a libretto of his own, which shows that he is a satirist of very wide range, with whose deeper thoughts, musical and other, we shall have to reckon.

I shall not dwell on the humour of these variations, nor shall I quote the theme. The listener will be well advised to take the whole composition seriously as a thing admirable in general design, full of contrasts, and rich in beautiful melodic ideas of the composer's own. I see in it none of the commonplaces into which a facile writer would fall if his notion of musical humour were confined to the dressing up of a nursery rhyme in learned terms. It need not fear comparison with Dohnányi's masterpiece in the same kind.

I quote the human feminine element in the saga:

It seems, to judge from the later expansion of this melody, that the Muricide was of a nature to invite pursuit as well as to pursue. (In fact, the legend tells us that her victims pursued her.) I have not succeeded in identifying the Agriculturalist as an actor in this music-drama; and I have no reason to suppose that his jealousy introduced a human note into the tragedy. The final chorale is unquestionably a Requiem for the Three, and for no others.

ADOLF BUSCH

CCXLIX. CAPRICCIO FOR SMALL ORCHESTRA, OP. 46

Some day I may attempt to give an account, at large and in detail, of what I know of the work, careers, and characters of the brothers Fritz and Adolf Busch. To me it has been profoundly interesting to see how two younger artists who never knew Joachim are spontaneously repeating, after an interval of some eighty years, many typical processes in that great man's development. One is never quite sure of having attained a completely detached view of one's own upbringing; and few thrills are more rejuvenating than the discovery that one's loyalties have been given not only to certain persons, but to the things those persons represented; that one's own world has been no home of impossible loyalties and lost causes, but a climate of bracing reality for younger artists.

Among modern composers the chief influences on Adolf Busch have been Reger, the dominating influence from his earliest days, and Busoni, the friend of his maturity. These composers differ widely from Joachim and from each other in racial type and general outlook, but all three have in common the most obvious feature of their style. This I believe the criticism of our day would call its 'intellectuality'; but I am not very sure of my capacity to understand contemporary criticism, and I have an uneasy suspicion that this term means something which the critic does not like. What is certain is that neither Reger nor Busoni suffered fools gladly. Joachim was more patient. No two people have the same sense of humour. I am not sure that Reger's has much ground in common with Busoni's; but I think I can see my way about Adolf Busch's, which certainly can hold its ground independently of both the elder composers. This Capriccio could be analysed as a structure of classical counterpoint and harmony—and the analysis would be quite interesting to students, inasmuch as the counterpoint really is classical—that is to say, it is harmony. The harmony is produced by the counterpoint; a quite different process from that of playing several different themes simultaneously and calling the resulting casual misfits harmonic freedom. The disadvantage alleged against the classical procedure is that 'you can't hear it'; when the combination really harmonizes, the individual themes vanish, except for the topmost. But perhaps this is one of the real meanings of the adage about the art of concealing art. Anyhow it seems more definite than to suppose that art is to artist as bone to dog, and that round Sirius there revolves some Platonic planet containing a garden where all the highest art lies concealed.[1]

And yet that supposition has attractions for me at the present moment. Readers of my notes, aware of my propensity to attach external 'programmes' to the most absolute music, will appreciate how much more readable I could make my analysis of Busch's Capriccio if I were permitted to call the work *A Dog-Fight in*

---

[1] Some colour is given to this theory by the fact, revealed by recent astrophysics, that actually in the companion or satellite of Sirius matter is thousands of times more dense than anything known under terrestrial conditions.

Sirius and to display my knowledge of such events without further attention to the music. Whatever is not known of such events, it is at least certain that they are very funny, and they cannot be more difficult to describe than the humour of absolute music. However, dogmatism (the enharmonic modulation is unintentional) must suffice for my account of Busch's Capriccio. There is extant an old German play-bill of a tragedy which gives notice that '*Das Lachen ist verboten, da es ein Trauerspiel ist*'. This capriccio is not a tragedy, and unless I am grievously mistaken, you are not forbidden to laugh in the right places. They are, of course, the places which make *me* laugh. But to point them out would be but a variant of the psychological error of the old play-bill.

Nevertheless I shall take the precaution of remarking that there is nothing funny about the beauty of the mysterious introductory adagio. The beauty is, of course, the foundation of all the humour; and the humour is perfectly compatible with the return of the adagio in a passage near the end of the work. Another harmonious element in this return is the fact that the adagio is and remains mysterious: if it had been more concrete or formal its return might have had a tinge of sentimentality or tub-thumpery; and against either of these qualities the atmosphere of Busch's art is the strongest of antiseptics.

The adagio announces a pair of themes—

Ex. 1.
Adagio.

8ve lower.

Ex. 2.
&c.

both of which will eventually take shape in the main body of the work. At present the key, F minor, is the harmonic antipodes of the B minor which is to become our tonic. Towards B minor the music drifts on a tide which is none the less cogent for its direction not being obvious; while the general tendency is that of a great crescendo. Of the two themes the more mobile, Ex. 2, soon combines contrapuntally with Ex. 1 over which it gradually gains the ascendancy. A tendency to accelerate becomes evident, but is checked, until with the imminence of the destined key of B minor, the restraint is removed.

The presto gives Ex. 2 as its main theme, in two versions, a tirade—

Ex. 3.

and a more formal measure.

Ex. 4.

As my figures show, Ex. 4 at first appears at a different rhythmic angle from Ex. 3; but this displacement turns out to be only an illusion resulting from an odd bar. The listener will hear many more subtle displacements of this theme by half a bar or even by a single crotchet. The whole work is polyphonic, even when not actually in fugue, and there is no predicting how and when its several themes will combine. Soon Ex. 1 sails in, beginning in its original F minor, now infinitely remote but drifting with surprising ease to our B minor within the length of its own phrase. A new theme, in close fugato, shows some pugnacity—

Ex. 5.

and with its development the Sirian warfare (if I may use my un-authorized analogy) is soon in full swing. But it collapses suddenly; and more complex strategies ensue in conspiratorial whispers in which old themes are busy around the following new figures.

Ex. 6.

The council of the conspirators is soon broken by sudden loud indiscretions, which lead to an outburst of Ex. 3, fortissimo in D major. This works up to a climax, from which there is another dramatic collapse into a quiet central episode beginning in C major. The tempo does not change, but the rhythm becomes so broad that I find the new melody best displayed by giving my quotation another time-signature so as to throw two bars into one.

Ex. 7.

With this episode the underlying romantic depth of the work appears on the surface. Perhaps I ought not to use the word 'romantic'. Long before modern art had definitely revolted from it, a great French critic, quoted by Matthew Arnold, had roundly declared that 'the romantic' was simply 'le faux'. And I confess to a violent dislike both of the term and the thing when conceived as in opposition to 'the classic'. But I have a not less violent objection to 'the classic' as conceived in such opposition; and when I use the word 'romantic' I beg to be understood as talking not history, but plain English. In plain English 'romantic' is just what this episode is, and it consists of not less adamantine fact than the rude remarks from Ex. 6, which eventually dispel it and lead to the return of Ex. 4 in a triumphant tonic major. Further developments of this, the main theme, now seem to go abroad again, Ex. 1 intervening in its own remote F minor; but the general tendency of all the modulations and new devices proves to be that of a peroration or coda, and the tonic asserts itself more and more, even though the final cadence of the work is a joke on the flat-supertonic topic (C natural to B). The reappearance of the actual tempo and material of the introductory adagio is as romantic as moonshine and as cosmic as Einstein; and the runaway end is as funny as the *x-te Streich* of the immortal creations of another Busch, Max and Moritz.

ZÁDOR

CCL. RONDO FOR ORCHESTRA

Eugen Zádor was born in 1895 at Bátászek, Hungary. He studied under Heuberger and Max Reger in Leipzig. Since 1922 he has been a Professor at the Conservatorium at Vienna. His works comprise songs, pianoforte works, chamber music, orchestral works of many kinds, operas, and ballets.

The Rondo for Orchestra is one of his latest works, being written in 1933. It has been already performed in almost every country except Great Britain. It admirably represents the style of a master who, being versed in every form of classical technique, has devised a pleasantly humorous *modus vivendi* with every modern tendency that does not display a conscientious objection to mastery.

The classical rondo form appears with crystal clarity in the alternations of the main theme—

with the two contrasted episodes—

the recapitulation of the first episode (Ex. 2) in the home tonic, and the final return of the main theme expanded into a coda.

But the most essentially classical feature of the whole work is its freedom in matters of detail. Nothing can be more clearly recognizable than the return of the main theme, and its various developments by diminution and other devices; but the appearance of regularity is as deceptive as in the mature style of Haydn. Ex. 1 shows only the first statement of the theme. On each return, the theme swings in at a different angle and at a different position, and is continued in some new and unpredictable way. Such facts should be mentioned, just because they do not at once strike the listener. Nor, indeed, is it necessary that they should; they are symptoms of a vitality that makes its own immediate impression, without displaying its mechanism. The quality upon which every listener will seize with avidity is the brilliant orchestration, in which Zádor's mastery is obvious even in an age and an environment in which all musicians are supposed to orchestrate brilliantly. But, as my old friend John Farmer used to say, many of the finest things in music seem playable with two clothes-pegs and a toothpick. Such resources would perhaps be inadequate for the execution of this Rondo. But on paper it presents a deceptive appearance of having been constructed out of the less ambitious of Czerny's 1,000,001 exercises. This the listener would not guess; and I do not advise him to believe in such appearances even when they are pointed out to him.

CCLI. WAGNER IN THE CONCERT-ROOM

In the middle of the nineteenth century there was one main reason why the teaching of musical composition fell into bad ways. This was the delusion that musical art-forms exist in a generalized state and can be grasped as in a bird's-eye view. In the later nineteenth century another delusion arose, and both are now prevalent. This other delusion arose from the persecution and the triumph of Wagner. Both the persecutors and the Wagnerians argued without knowledge of any genuine principles of musical composition, and both sides were in unconscious agreement that, whether Wagner could or could not compose, he did not, as a matter of fact, do so. It is as absurd and as essentially underbred to complain of the 'vogue' of Wagner as to complain of the 'vogue' of Beethoven. But extracts of Beethoven as accompaniments to cowpuncher films are not more artistic than Wagner concerts of selections which, like Mr. Punch's early classification of trains, consist of (a) those which start but do not arrive; (b) those which arrive but do not start; and (c) those which neither start nor arrive. With the vogue of such concerts and the approval of them by critics, the last vestiges of popular and academic instinct for composition disappeared. It has now been decided to ordain that Wagner shall be out of fashion. To this I move an amendment. Let it be decided that Wagner is a composer; and that until the arbiters of musical fashion have shown themselves capable of recognizing the difference between a composition and a scrap-book the public that goes to hear Wagner's music-dramas shall be allowed to enjoy its normal and healthy activity of understanding Wagner's music through his drama without fear or favour of fashion. How grave the destruction of all critical and academic standards of composition has become through the acceptance of inartistic Wagner excerpts may be seen from a recent example when a highly educated writer on music contributed to a musical journal some interesting and important remarks upon the prelude to *Tristan*, in which he assumed that in the concert-room it was inseparable from the *Liebestod*, and accordingly had no complete key-system. No doubt to the general public key-systems are academic technicalities which concern only teachers of harmony. Similarly, to repeat one of my favourite illustrations, the distinction between the nominative and accusative is an affair for grammarians. But the general public will miss something of material interest to it if the translators and producers of a tragedy in a foreign language do not know who killed whom; and a piece without a key-system or with an incoherent key-system does not give the naïve listener the same coherent impression, or even the same tuneful impression, as he will get, without any knowledge of theory, from a piece that has a key in which it begins and ends. Now the excellent critic who wrote so well about the prelude-and-liebestod monstrosity betrayed that he did not know that Wagner wrote a page, one of the most beautiful in all his works, that finishes the prelude in its proper key and makes it as coherent and as exact in its proportions as any movement by Bach. The critic was thus quite unaware that the modulations which lead to the rise of the curtain upon the first act are a powerful and subtle dramatic catastrophe in their proper place.

This orthodox view of Wagner's later style is no better than a conviction that Wagner's mind was a mush. Here we see a reverential Wagnerian actually unaware that Wagner did his best, and an absolutely perfect best, to make the *Tristan* Vorspiel a coherent piece of music in A minor ending in A major, with a sense of tonality strengthened, instead of being weakened, by what has been happily called his 'chromatic iridescence' at its highest power. Most unfortunately, it happens that the catastrophic darkening to C minor upon which the curtain rises at the beginning of the play makes a grammatically correct join with the dark chords from which Isolde's dying utterances emerge into a key not only different from, but totally destructive of the harmonic basis of the prelude. What do we gain by joining these two pieces in the concert-room? For those who know the whole music-drama we gain the opportunity of listening to a quotation from the end of the opera after we have heard the uncompleted prelude. We can, if we like, imagine that the rest of the three acts are past. But we do not gain the living or dying presence of Isolde herself, because the problem of how to represent the voice-part in a purely instrumental performance is solved by the sublimely simple process of leaving it out. Liszt, in his wonderful transcription of the *Liebestod* for pianoforte, did not go quite so far, inasmuch as he contrived to represent no less than seven independent vocal notes and a grace-note near the beginning: *seht ihr's Freunde? Seht ihr's nicht?* For the rest, it is a remarkable symptom of an abnormality in Wagner's art that, though the voice inevitably dominates the attention whenever it is heard among instruments, and though the vocal writing of Isolde's *Liebestod* is perfect both in declamation and singability, it is so little essential to Wagner's invention that Isolde's *Liebestod* is a complete piece of music without Isolde at all. She is singing for sixty-eight bars, and in twenty-five of these she is able to deliver the main theme, constantly broken, sometimes quite awkwardly, by pauses and other necessities of declamation. For the other forty-three bars she is descanting in counterpoints, of which, as I have already remarked, Liszt has been able to preserve seven notes and a grace-note. How much of these counterpoints does any one, except the singer, remember? Surely her last notes should be memorable? They are the right notes in the right declamation; they easily penetrate the orchestra, and they will do justice to the most golden of voices. How many music-lovers can quote them? They have never been heard in the concert-room, except when a singer was engaged; but I should not be surprised if many of the music-lovers who go to every stage performance of *Tristan* found themselves unable to quote them.

If we wish to use Isolde's *Liebestod* in the concert-room as a quotation, just as we might enjoy an eminent actor reciting a soliloquy from Shakespeare, we cannot object to doing the *Liebestod* without Isolde. It is no case of Hamlet without the Prince of Denmark. The only possible objection to playing the *Liebestod* as an instrumental piece is that it begins nowhere. Liszt's pianoforte transcription remedies this by four magnificently powerful and subtle introductory bars which ought obviously to be used in the orchestral version. For the rest, not only is the *Liebestod* a mere quotation in the concert-room, but it owes most of its power in the opera itself to the fact that it is there a quotation from the love-duet in the second act. That is one reason why Isolde's vocal part in it is so fragmentary. In the original duet both she and Tristan are much more centred upon the real themes of the music.

Busoni argued the case for Wagner excerpts. He objected strongly to Wagner on various grounds of taste, some of which we may regard as indisputable in the Horatian sense. Horace was a wise man whose guiding principle in life was to avoid causes of irritation; and no stupidity irritates me so much as the intelligence which sees so instantly through everything that it has no time to see into anything. Swift noted with admiration the use of a special blunt-edged knife that could cut folded paper safely and neatly, whereas more acute instruments would leave the crease. The interesting point in Busoni's defence of concert-room extracts of Wagner lies in his complaint that the emotional concentration of such music, added to the effect of stage action and poetry, becomes intolerable when presented as Wagner intended, but is acceptable when diluted and dosed out as elegant extracts in the concert-room. This argument begins to concern us when we have some idea of what Wagner is driving at; but in the present state of knowledge as represented by a popular Wagner concert it is far above our heads, for the people who can accept such concert-pieces as the *Walkürenritt* and *Waldweben* attach no more emotional or intellectual ideas to these extracts than they attach to whisky. The exciting sensuous quality of Wagner's music—and not only of Wagner's, but of any music—may become as bad for them as the exciting sensuous quality of whisky; and they will not long be able even to keep up appearances as persons of discriminating taste. The expert wine-taster must take care to be a sober man.

I have before me a collection of the most usual Wagner concert-room excerpts, and propose to describe some of them. First, as a matter of principle, let us be quite clear that there can be no objection to producing large scenes from Wagner's operas upon the concert platform with singers, but without scenery and costumes. We know that we are listening to dramatic scenes, and we gain as much by hearing them with unfatigued attention as we lose by the self-evident fact that these scenes are fragments. I should not have the slightest objection to covering most of the ground of Wagner's music-dramas in concert-room performances of whole scenes with singers. In this way I have enjoyed at a Leeds festival the end of *Siegfried*, beginning with the passage of Siegfried through the fire, and have felt myself rather than the conditions to blame for any feeling of absurdity when music which represented Siegfried as setting the sleeping Brünnhilde free from the burden of her armour could receive no illustration from the deportment of a lady and gentleman standing up in evening dress on the platform. Together with a financial licence for performing the complete works of Berlioz and Mahler, I should like nothing better than the opportunity to take the Reid Orchestra on such terms through everything of Wagner that they ought to know, and I should think that I was participating in educating the public for a better appreciation of the dramatic, as well as the musical, values of Wagner's art by an all-comprehending series of such concerts. But I cannot speak too strongly in condemnation of some of the most popular concert-pieces that have been carved from Wagner's works. Even some of the vocal ones are miserably scrappy, and seem almost deliberately calculated to reveal weaknesses which in the magnificent flow of the drama would pass unnoticed by any one with a sense of proportion, Siegmund's love-song from the *Walküre* (*Winterstürme wichen dem Wonnemond*) comes at one of the supremely poetic moments in the first act of *Walküre*. Wagner's bitterest enemies have confessed themselves overwhelmed by the poetic beauty of the moment when the doors of Hunding's house fly open and reveal the moonlight that has followed upon the departure of the storm. The accepted concert extract misses this moment and confines itself to Siegmund's tune, which begins well, but taken by itself reveals certain weaknesses from which Wagner's more sustained melodies are seldom free; it then carries the tune as far as Siegmund can carry it, and adds an orchestral cadence which finishes the business with a bump. In its proper context the slight local weaknesses of the melody are negligible, and the whole passage begins to take shape with a glorious flow when Sieglinde takes it up in the same tempo, but in a broader musical metre. I could greatly enjoy the whole act without scenery, and I should have no objection to beginning half-way through, where Siegmund has been left alone to reflect by the firelight upon his desperate plight, before Sieglinde re-enters to tell him of the sword awaiting his grasp in the trunk of the very tree which supports his enemy's house where he is sitting. In such an extract it would be pedantic to detect a weakness in a few bars of Siegmund's spring-song.

The *Walkürenritt* is more effective, and for that very reason considerably worse. In the drama it comes with sublime effect after the human tragedy seems over. Siegmund is slain in spite of Brünnhilde's attempt to protect him, and the disobedient Valkyrie has rescued Sieglinde and fled from the wrath of Wotan. The curtain rises upon the third act, and we are on mountain heights among the storm clouds, far away from human tragedies, watching the personified storm clouds assembling as Valkyries riding through the air bearing the souls of slain warriors to become Wotan's garrison in Valhalla. But what is the use of describing all this to an audience which is going to hear nothing but a scrap of orchestral fireworks that fails to achieve any musical form and yet lasts too long for its musical content? The *Walkürenritt*, as chopped off for concert purposes, spends twelve bars in establishing a galloping rhythm beneath a continued vibration punctuated by noises like the discharge of rockets. The noises and the galloping rhythm continue beneath a good broad sequential theme moving in four-bar steps with four-bar pauses. With necessary repetitions, this is built up into two statements, the second of which achieves some emphasis by ending on a sudden tonic major chord. At this point the curtain should rise, but of course in the concert-room nothing happens. The *Ho-jo-to-ho* of the Valkyries, one of the most thrilling war-cries ever devised by a musician, suggests nothing as an instrumental formula; and all that remains for the naïve listener in the concert-room is to wonder why the whole bundle of sequences merely repeats itself some three or four times with the same climaxes and then ends with a bump. What people enjoy in the *Walkürenritt* as a concert-piece is an orchestral firework which is neither more nor less than vulgar; but the vulgarity is not Wagner's. One of the main types of vulgarity consists in effects without causes. Here you have a set of effects which originally had perfect dramatic causes. There is accurate gradation in the arrival sometimes of one Valkyrie, sometimes of two, and of the heightened expectation of the arrival of Brünnhilde, the cause of whose delay is known to the audience but not to the Valkyries. Wagner is tied to his monotonous key region by reasons self-evident on the time scale not only of the drama, but of the music itself. Thanks to the vulgarizing of the *Walkürenritt* as a cheap and nasty orchestral firework, our up-to-date anti-Wagnerians, including Busoni himself, listen to Wagner even on the stage with ears trained to accept the abysmal ignorance of composition that has been inculcated by these misrepresentations of him in the concert-room.

The *Walkürenritt* degrades a sublime episode into a vulgar firework, but does not reach the grovelling imbecility of the extract from *Siegfried* known as *Waldweben*. In the second act of *Siegfried* the hero, having been guided to the cave where the dragon Fafner lurks, is for a while left alone by his treacherous guide and foster-father, Mime. He spends the time in delightful speculations as to his origin and destiny and in listening to the song of the birds, which he wishes he could understand. He tries to imitate the bird-songs by piping on a reed which he plucks and cuts on the spur of the moment. Finding the resources of his pipe (or of the cor anglais in the orchestra) insufficient, he begins a tune on an instrument he knows better, his hunting-horn. This calls up a response from Fafner the dragon; and in the ensuing dialogue the tactlessness of the interlocutors ends fatally for Fafner, whose dying utterances reveal something, but not enough, to Siegfried as to his destiny. In pulling his sword from Fafner's body Siegfried's hand is stung by the dragon's blood, and when he puts it to his lips the taste of the blood magically reveals to him not only the language of the birds, but the real meaning of all that the treacherous Mime has to say to him. Consequently, the song of the birds is from this point

represented by the voice of an invisible singer telling Siegfried of
the Ring and the Tarnhelm, warning him against Mime, and revealing to him that a bride awaits him on a fire-encircled mountain.
There are a few other incidents, such as a quarrel between Mime
and his elder brother Alberich. Then there is the slaying of Mime
by Siegfried as the inevitable climax of a dialogue in which the
audience as well as Siegfried hear with the insight conveyed by the
dragon's blood the real intention of Mime disguised in the flatteries
with which he offers the hero a poisonous brew to refresh him.
Siegfried is then so lonely that he almost regrets this; but the bird
tells him of the bride that awaits him on the fire-encircled rock and
flies before him to show him the way.

In order to enjoy the second act of *Siegfried*, I do not feel the
need of Wagner's naïvely illusionistic Bayreuth scenery, and still
less do I desire the interference of some of the modern forms of
inattention which are foisted on Wagner's dramas by our severer
Disillusionists; but I know few things sillier than the concert-
piece known as *Waldweben*. In their place Wagner's bird-song
themes are charming, and beautifully balanced between pure orchestral music and the necessary but quite unrealistic suggestion of
actual birds. But we do not want to hear them built up twice into
nothing in particular. This *Waldweben* extract begins harmonically nowhere, at the only point at which some means can be found
for leading to Siegfried's meditations about his parentage. These
meditations have to be boiled down into an affair with neither structure nor contrasts; and then the bird-song figures are given, also
without structure or contrasts, some three times. (It is impossible
to count precisely with piles of Wagner's inherently self-repetitive
expanses.) Anyhow, there is nothing left but bird-song, uninter-
rupted by Fafner or Mime. But one problem remains: how is
Wagner, or his arranger, to represent the difference made by the
dragon's blood? Why, what could be more self-evident and thrilling than to add a glockenspiel? As soon as the notes are thus
invested with the surprising moisture of a chocolate which you
have crunched before you knew that it contained a liqueur, the
miracle is accomplished, and one of Wagner's most poetic scenes
has been reduced to an even sillier triviality than the concert
Walkürenritt.

I am, as I have insisted elsewhere, entirely in favour of giving
whole acts, or *final* scenes (not middle scenes), in the concert-
room, with the requisite singers. Wotan's Farewell in *Walküre*, and
Brünnhilde's last scene in *Götterdämmerung*, for instance, with no
cuts in the orchestral sequels, are intelligible musical propositions
which carry dramatic meaning wherever they are produced. But
Siegfried's funeral march, out of its context, is nonsense. The

annotator or critic who calls it a marvellous piece of musical texture and composition might as well apply the same praise to the pictorial values of the 'cloud-clock', or steam jets, or the ordinary curtain, or whatever means are taken to cover the change of scene. The funeral march in *Götterdämmerung* is *part* of a marvellous piece of texture and composition, but that marvellous piece has taken most of four days to reach the beginning of the march. And if you must take one triglyph and two blocks of masonry as constituting a sample of a monument you could hardly make a worse selection than this funeral march. Of its four main themes (I exclude the so-called Death-theme as a mere descriptive gesture) two are among Wagner's most obvious lapses. In the vast achievement of the *Ring* they matter far less than a single perfunctory coloratura in one of Handel's greatest works; but if we are to regard such a fragment as this funeral march as an independent composition, it is a serious defect that one of its main themes should be the very awkward and mechanical transformation of Siegfried's juvenile horn-theme into a sophisticated grown-up affair in learned syncopations, and that another should be the theme of Brünnhilde as a mortal woman, a theme which descends markedly below Weber's most suburban (*spiessbürgerlich*) style. In a decent performance of *Götterdämmerung* these lapses are more negligible than a line like 'Flies may do this, but I from this must fly' in *Romeo and Juliet*; and not less negligible from the fact that they are irremovably imbedded in the whole structure. There was a time when Hamlet's Soliloquy had its place along with Cato's in volumes of Elegant Extracts. Dr. Johnson was compelled to hear Cato's Soliloquy recited by a little girl who proved not only ignorant of the meaning of the words 'bane' and 'antidote' but unable to tell how many pence there were in sixpence. No doubt the lexicographical manner was alarming to one so young. But there are plenty of people not so very young who would be the better of something alarming when they start a fashion of abusing, or even patronizing, Wagner on the basis of their vast experience as concert-goers, enlarged later in life by the discovery that Wotan and King Marke are tedious; a discovery which is far more jejune than honest George the Third's observation that much of Shakespeare is sad stuff, and which lacks the royal common sense which inspired that under-rated monarch to add 'but one must not say so'. We no longer try to appreciate Hamlet's soliloquy as an independent poem. It is not so fragmentary as the funeral march in *Götterdämmerung*; and for such *disjecta membra* in music the difference is negligible between the genuine article and the version of the two rapscallions in *Huckleberry Finn*, which began

To be or not to be, that is the bare bodkin

and ended

> But soft! the fair Ophelia!
> Ope not thy ponderous and marble jaws,
> But get thee to a nunnery; hence! away!

A Good-Friday concert is considered orthodox if, and only if, it contains the *Charfreitagszauber* from *Parsifal*. At the end of the nineteenth century, when the dawn of British musical criticism was represented by the vitriolic attacks which writers of brilliant English in the *Saturday Review* and the *Star* directed against Stanford and Parry and any other musician who was guilty of holding an official post, this Good-Friday music from *Parsifal* was often adduced as an example of music which held its own in the concert-room on its pure musical merits in spite of all that Wagner himself said against the practice of representing him by such fragments, I had often heard it myself as a concert-piece, and have no reason to believe that I saw less of its purely musical beauty than did the late J. F. Runciman of the *Saturday Review*; but when I first heard *Parsifal* at Bayreuth I noticed with some amusement that the Good-Friday music in its proper place did not strike a familiar chord at all. Not only did it mean all that was implied and explained by its position in the drama, but it became a piece of quite sensible music, instead of a piece of orchestration beginning nowhere in particular, repeating its figures, like all unsound Wagner extracts, far too often for variety, obstinately refusing to change its ground when change of ground is musically due, making no effort towards a climax unless a belated one conscious of its untimeliness, and ending vaguely from exhaustion in a region which, like that of the beginning, is nowhere in particular, but different inasmuch as it is elsewhere. If your notion of music is that of Charles Lamb in his famous Essay on Ears, you may or may not like 'sugar piled upon honey' better than he did; but you and the late Mr. Runciman will be well advised to refrain from attacking as 'proud academics' such patient and faithful servants of music for its own sake as Stanford and Parry.

The *Charfreitagszauber* is not as stupidly disconnected an extract of *Parsifal* as the *Waldweben* is of *Siegfried*, but there is a version of it that reaches what we may hope to be the lowest and most elaborate stupidity that has been attained in concert-music since the days when the flute was a fashionable instrument for gentlemen, and Handel's *Hallelujah* Chorus was published in an arrangement for two flutes representing four-part harmony by grace-notes. Some years ago, one of the world's leading orchestras gave two concerts in London, one of which was a real concert, and the other was a Wagner night. It was a condition of etiquette that the leader of the orchestra should play a solo, and there was no room for this in the genuine concert; and he accordingly was allowed, or even encouraged, to spend a quarter of an hour of the Wagner night in playing Wilhelmj's arrangement of the Good-Friday music as a violin solo. That is to say, the first-rate leader of a first-rate orchestra, with the connivance of the conductor, consummated the iniquities of the perpetrator of Bach's *Air on the G String* by publicly performing a version of the Good-Friday music which added to the horrors of its mutilated condition the process of draining it of all orchestral colour except in its accompaniments. Wilhelmj substituted, for every tone in the melody of voices, strings, and wind, a uniform whitewash of high and thin solo violin tone with nothing resembling violin style, until the climax where the glorious tone of the *tutti* strings made the poor solo player everlastingly ridiculous by answering him with his own phrase at the same pitch. How the distinguished leader of a distinguished orchestra could consent to make such a fool of himself is as incomprehensible as that the conductor could touch such an arrangement with a pair of tongs.

The scope for Wagner concerts is wide if singers can be engaged and time found for the inclusion of whole scenes that comprise a definite dramatic or poetic entity. Without voices the scope is so restricted that I doubt whether more than two concerts could be given of which the programmes did not overlap. The following programme almost exhausts the possibilities of a 'legitimate' Wagner concert without voices:

1. OVERTURE to *Der Fliegende Holländer*.
2. PRELUDE to Act III of *Tannhäuser* (Tannhäuser's Pilgrimage), in the Original Version.
3. VENUSBERG MUSIC.
4. VORSPIEL to LOHENGRIN.

Interval.

5. A FAUST OVERTURE.
6. SIEGFRIED IDYLL.
7. VORSPIEL to *Tristan und Isolde*.
8. KAISERMARSCH.

The overture to *Der Fliegende Holländer* is excellent as a musical whole and immeasurably riper than any other part of the opera. The introduction to the third act of *Tannhäuser* is interesting in its original version, published long after Wagner's death and rejected by him as redundant in the opera. It comprises the whole of Tannhäuser's narrative, and thus amounts to an instrumental piece of which the contents are emotionally complete; for which very reason it would weaken the effect of Tannhäuser's narrative later on. The Venusberg Ballet holds an extraordinary position in Wagner's works. Every one with a sense of integrity in style will agree with Weingartner in pleading that the opera of *Tannhäuser* should be given in its native crudeness according to Wagner's first ideas. When his fame had been established beyond the power of Parisian and international hostilities, he attached enough importance to the possibility of a triumph in Paris to acquiesce in the local etiquette that demanded opportunity for the Parisian *corps-de-ballet*. The opening scene in the Venusberg was the only place where a ballet could be inserted, and he wrote one in his ripest style. He also confessed that his original 'Venus of the coulisses' horrified his mature taste, and so he rewrote her share of the dialogue in a musical language as ripe as that of Isolde. But poor Tannhäuser was past praying for. His famous song, and his whole share in the scene, hardly acquits itself better in these surroundings than the Tichborne Claimant. The ballet itself can neither by position nor substance achieve any important dramatic meaning. In order to make room for it, the contest of singers in the Wartburg, to which the opera owes its sub-title and half its dramatic importance, has had to be so shortened that Tannhäuser has no time to develop a gradual crescendo of his tragic opposition to the ascetic minstrels, but must act as under demoniac possession from the outset. Every musician must agree with Weingartner that the Venusberg Ballet is on the one hand destructive to the opera of *Tannhäuser*, and on the other a highly effective concert-piece. But this is not all. We hear it year in and year out tacked on to the overture, as Wagner himself tacked it on for the Paris Opera. In this condition it is a monster without its Loch Ness. Nobody can tell how many humps it has, nor what purpose they serve. The overture to *Tannhäuser* is a mixture of the best and worst things in Wagner's early style. It is ripest where it is naughty—that is to say, in its Venusberg elements; it is blotchy and feeble in Tannhäuser's song; and where it means to be holy and humble it is predestined to a Moody-and-Sankey tub-thumping end, and of that end I would not see it deprived. As a whole it is not good music, but it is very good bad music. When the naughty Venusberg music of Wagner's mature style encroaches upon it, the result is that the overture, instead of naïvely fulfilling its honest destiny as a piece of rather bad edifying music, proceeds to develop its naughty elements in a very much better style than it had ever dreamed of before. But the new climaxes do not rise from their own basis. They have been exhausted by two or three cruder climaxes of the same kind. No doubt it is well that the Moody-and-Sankey elements should disappear. There is no humour in their being discountenanced by all this wicked superiority; but why put up with such a squalid misalliance at all? It was a revelation to me when I first took the Venusberg Ballet by itself and realized that Wagner had achieved a perfect composition, of which the climaxes are exactly as many as are necessary, and the decline to exhaustion is entirely beautiful and perfectly proportioned. As printed, the ballet is a little indefinite in its beginning: enough so to make a plausible case for drifting into it from the overture; but a tradition, the origin of which I cannot trace, has added two bars to the printed opening which throw the whole thing into a shape hardly less perfect than that of the *Tristan* Vorspiel as Wagner ended it.

The *Lohengrin* Vorspiel is another piece which is entirely admirable by itself and immeasurably riper than anything in the opera. Joachim, as inveterate an anti-Wagnerian as ever refrained from joining in controversies, always expressed the greatest admiration for it, and overrode all opposition to including it in the repertoire of his Hochschule students. On the other hand, I have no use for the prelude to the third act of *Lohengrin*, which relapses very successfully into Wagner's vulgarest early style and fizzles out more ineptly than most fragments. I would not mind swallowing it in its proper function as a prelude to the very pretty bridal march which, with singular disregard for ominous associations, replaces our beloved Mendelssohn's march in American weddings.

The other pieces in this programme are obviously not theatre music. The *Siegfried Idyll* is connected with *Siegfried* only by thematic links which amount to hardly more than quotations privately current in a family because their connexion with their source is jocular; yet some of our new anti-Wagnerians pose as serious critics and call this most important of all Wagner's instrumental works an operatic pot-pourri.

The *Faust* Overture I have often performed, and have analysed fairly fully in Vol. IV of these essays.

Irresponsible writers have latterly held up the *Kaisermarsch* to contempt: presumably on political grounds that are more worthy of elderly eggs than of human beings. No person who has read or heard the *Kaisermarsch* need imagine that he has the smallest claims to musical culture if he cannot see that it is a composition of the highest order and the noblest style. Even in the dawn of imperial Germany for which it was written, Wagner did not expect that there would be many occasions in which its concluding *Volksgesang* could be actually sung by audiences, however carefully the text and notes were distributed amongst them; and he was too wise to make this consummation an essential part of his musical scheme, though no doubt the final element of community singing would add greatly to the effect. I refrain from quoting the text, which is neither better nor worse than is to be expected from patriotic poetry written for a nation that could not disguise its satisfaction at having recently walloped a neighbouring nation; but its boast is modest compared with the claims and powers of the humblest dictators of modern times, and I see no reason why politics should interfere with the integrity of this grand specimen of Wagner's music at this time of day.

CCLII. THE VENUSBERG MUSIC ('TANNHÄUSER')

Wagner himself is responsible for the bad effect of welding his magnificent and mature Venusberg music on to his crude *Tannhäuser* Overture. His temptation was overwhelming, for he was at the height of his fame, and the occasion was his opportunity for generously allowing Paris to rehabilitate its reputation after the riot with which its Jockey Club had ruined the production of *Tannhäuser* years before. And perhaps he did not himself realize how effectively his own mature style ruins the rest of *Tannhäuser*. The only position for a single ballet in that drama is at the opening, before the action has begun: the work is already dangerously long and quite incapable of digesting two ballets; and to have dancers in the decorum of the Landgrave's Hall of Song would be absurdly incongruous with any restriction of their share in the orgies of the Venusberg. The result is that the Venusberg ballet has no dramatic significance at all. Neither, for that matter, has 70 per cent. of the ballet-music of Gluck; most of it has to be explained into the dramas by the choreographers.

The Paris bacchanale replaces a cruder affair that serves to set the scene and pose the actors in the original version of *Tannhäuser*. In the immense grottoes of the Hörselberg Tannhäuser is lying at the feet of Venus, who, knowing that his longing for a return to earthly daylight will soon transcend her power to retain him, is watching with some anxiety the growing frenzy of other denizens of her realm. Both in the perfunctory original ballet and in the mature Paris version, the frenzy of the dancers shocks the goddess's sense of decorum; and at her command a posse of her winged archers discharge narcotic arrows at the dancers, who subside into languorous slumbers.

The original *Tannhäuser* ballet followed the overture, and made an excellent contrast to its Moody-and-Sankey end. The Paris ballet was tacked on by Wagner himself to the overture just after the recapitulation of its crudest passage, Tannhäuser's song, with the result that three passages of Venusberg naughtiness in the overture forestall and destroy all appetite for the perfectly balanced scheme of the new ballet, which I myself am now hearing for the first time in its musical integrity. Its only discoverable defect as a detached piece is that, as printed, it begins nowhere; but either some authentic tradition or the inspiration of a conductor who understands composition has removed this defect by the addition of two bars of Ex. 1 in a manuscript slip inserted in the hired orchestral material.

Exx. 1 and 2 are common to the original and the Parisian ballet.

Ex. 1.

Ex. 2.

Ex. 3 is Parisian and is developed in Wagner's ripest style.

Ex. 3.

Exx. 4 and 5 are ripened from the original *Tannhäuser*, and show the goddess herself, here arising in annoyance at the riot and giving orders for it to be allayed.

Ex. 4.

Ex. 5.

Ex. 6 is a song of the sirens, which is the most thrilling feature both of the original and of the Parisian ballets.

Ex. 6.

Naht euch dem Strand - - el!

Voices are needed to give it its full effect; but to bring these into the concert-room would commit us to the whole scene in which, while Wagner has rewritten his *Kulissen-Venus* into the divinest style of Isolde, he has left poor Tannhäuser's song in its original ragged bumptiousness.

Although the defects of Wagner's early style are sufficiently Meyerbeerish to account for his aversion to that master in particular, it would be fairer to compare them with the style of a more disappointed master, Spontini. The mixture of styles is distressing in any version of *Tannhäuser* as a whole. Might we be forgiven for claiming that the original unadulterated opera has at all events the virtue of 'Spontineity'?

According to the Paris ballet, in the magnificent slow movement that follows upon Venus's orders the song of the sirens introduces two tableaux, representing two of Jupiter's adventures: as the bull that carries off Europa, and as the swan with Leda. Both as music and as drama, these matters are neither here nor there; though the text informs us that both were classical examples of the power of love. What concerns the listener is the exquisite development of another new theme in Wagner's ripest style, 'conflated' with Ex. 3—

which brings the movement to its musically appointed close. The last appearance of Ex. 1 indicates, as in the original ballet, how the troop of archers bow to Venus, signifying that they have succeeded in quelling the riot. The faint suggestion of church bells that haunts Tannhäuser's dreams of earthlight is accompanied by Wagner's new theme (Ex. 7) as the music dies away in its appointed time.

CCLIII. 'KAISERMARSCH'

Let us listen to the *Kaisermarsch* as a piece of music no more to be degraded by politics than Beethoven's *Weihe des Hauses*. To put it on the same level would be an error akin to the opposite extreme of criticism which rejects the *Weihe des Hauses*. The *Kaisermarsch* is not of that supreme order of subtlety and sublimity; but it has nothing to fear from the presence of Beethoven at his greatest: and its style is quite as useful as any Arnoldian 'touchstone of poetry' for the purpose of revealing the poverty of weaker music. Its

scheme anticipates Sibelius's idea of displaying fragments of
themes in an inchoate way, and reserving for the final climax their
gathering-up into a complete tune. Here is Wagner's complete
tune—

with which the composition ends; but the beginning is not fragmentary. Wagner starts at once with the first eleven bars. The
phrase-rhythm, with its cumulative repetitions and its avoidance
of symmetry, promptly shows that beyond all questions of taste this
artist can compose. For my part, I do not understand how any
disputes of taste can arise on any point in this composition. I can
see nothing but the noblest music in it at every moment, and have
no more use for political prejudices about it than for the eggs by
which such prejudices are appropriately and practically symbo-
lized.

Wagner follows these first eleven bars by a running figure—

which in two processes—first on the tonic, then on the dominant—
turns this opening statement into an introduction ending on a
pause. Then the larger structure begins. Its analysis would need
an essay not less elaborate than my full discussion of the *Weihe des
Hauses* Overture, which cost me almost more labour than any of

my other essays. All I can do here is to tabulate its main incidents.
First there is a slow crescendo on a swinging 'left-right, left-right'
bass.

Ex. 3.

The first attempt at modulation is checked by the sublime impact of a single line of *Ein' feste Burg*—

Ex. 4.

Ein' feste Burg.

followed by fanfares and a continuation of Ex. 3 in the dominant.
This leads, by a parallel incident of modulation, to another impact
of *Ein' feste Burg* in the subdominant, thus closing into the tonic.
The fanfares thereupon conclude the matter and die away at
leisure. Then Ex. 3 is developed quietly on a large scale. Gradually
the harmony leaves its home tonics and flashes out into bright
remote keys.

Ex. 5.

The note of *das ewig Weibliche* appears in the Walter-and-Eva
stream of melody which ensues. Gradually the materials of Ex. 1
assert themselves, and its figure (*b*) shows a power of shining like
a rainbow in the remotest keys. The modulations eventually come
round to the subdominant; and the approach to the climax is then
indicated by a grand rising sequence developed from figure (*e*)
which penetrates the softer counterpoints above, and is at length
surmounted by a third quotation of *Ein' feste Burg* in A♭ followed
for the first and only time by its second line.

Ex. 6.

This closes with a grand interrupted cadence into the home-dominant upon which an adequate length of fanfare leads to the complete Volksgesang as given in Ex. 1. Musicians whose sense of composition has suffered from the various inept ways in which Wagnerian excerpts end either with a bump, an inexplicable fade-out, or a couple of exasperatingly conventional chords, will find more and more cause to admire the accuracy of the simple-seeming conventional fanfare and last chords of the *Kaisermarsch*; the sort of detail which Wagner and Beethoven may perhaps take in their stride, or may (as we know from some cases in Beethoven) attain through dozens of sketches, the last of which may have been the same as the first.

CCLIV. 'PARSIFAL', ACT III

My objections to concert-room extracts of Wagner do not apply to whole scenes given with all the singers. Much is lost by the absence of scenery and action; but for some listeners almost as much is gained. The listener who has the intelligence to appreciate the loss will also have the imagination to supply what is missing, and may even find himself free from aesthetic discomforts that are inseparable from all efforts to present Wagner on the stage. There is not much to be said for people whose minds rise superior to any wish to see Wagner or Shakespeare acted. People who will not put up with reasonable, practical compromises may just as well confess that they do not want to put up with life. We may all wish that we knew what Shakespeare's audiences knew, but, while we should be the better for the sum of that knowledge, we should probably be the worse on the whole for being transformed into Elizabethan groundlings or Elizabethan aristocrats. Wagner is nearer to our own time; and those of us who can best appreciate his music can probably recognize that in matters concerning the stage his aesthetic sensibilities were less highly developed than his musical sense. Of the new highbrow anti-Wagnerian fashion I have no more to say than I have of the Edwardian anti-Beethoven reaction. Wagner's mature style fought its way upward from squalid antecedents with a force of character and an instinct for purity unsurpassed by the masters whose salad-days gave them no cause for regret. His detestation of the style of Meyerbeer was intensified by his recognition that his own early style was not without affinity to it. This did not prevent him from acknowledging in the most generous terms such good things as the end of the fourth act of *Les Huguenots*. With all his unscrupulous egotism, he was no snob. The anti-Wagnerians of the present-day have discovered with small labour and research that Wagner's style, like

most operatic styles, arose from squalid origins. They have discovered nothing else, and they proclaim from the housetops their
inability to distinguish between Wagner and Meyerbeer. '*Non
ragionam di lor, ma guarda e passa.*'

It is permissible to find in Wagner's temperament, as in Dante's,
Milton's, Carlyle's, Henry VIII's, and Queen Elizabeth's, much
that one dislikes; and it is nobody's duty in life to go in deliberate
search of diets that one knows to be beyond one's digestion. In
Wagner's lifetime there was something more than mere respect-
ability in the cause of the anti-Wagnerites. To-day we can see that
the musical language of *Tristan* is a rigorously logical, and even
conservative, extension of the principles of classical tonality and
harmony, arising naturally from the extension of the whole time-
scale of music. To most of Wagner's contemporaries that language
was unintelligible in its grammar, and very upsetting in its effect
upon the listener's nerves. So great a musician as Joachim went to
his grave in the twentieth century firmly convinced that the musical
language of *Tristan* was nonsensical as well as morbid. And the
musicians who knew that this was the result of their best efforts to
construe it were wiser than the people who saw no difficulty
in it at all. Their scepticism was based on a conviction, strongly
held by Wagner himself, that his earlier work contained much that
was not worthy of his ideals and was most popular where it least
represented them. The modern anti-Wagnerian is either an artist
so preoccupied with his own work that he resents even the most
unquestioned classics if their systems conflict with it, or he is a
dilettante who has drifted into music through current literature
and cannot construe anything whatever. No reasonable person
would expect Debussy to enjoy Wagner, or Berlioz to enjoy Bach.
We want such artists to get on with their own work, and we do not
see why they should be asked to listen to what disturbs them. But
I frankly own that my social tact will never be equal to meeting
with urbanity the anti-Wagnerian table-talk of the present day.
At its best it represents a natural inability to enjoy music on a
time-scale enormously larger than anything to which the listener
has been trained. Great artists like Vernon Lee and Maurice Baring
earn our gratitude by describing accurately the almost physical dis-
comfort they experience by having their attention racked by the
Wagnerian time-scale. But no illumination is given by gossip
repeated at second-hand by people who have overheard the reactionary utterances of sensitive artists. The popular taste—and, for
that matter, the fashionable taste—of those who are in a position,
geographical and financial, to go to operas, is far in advance of
critical fashions. Wagner continues to draw full houses because
his dramas are among the most exciting that have been realized

on the stage, and are the foundation of a music that has revealed the meaning of that art to persons who in former times never ventured to think themselves musical. He is one of the non-musicians' composers; and, by a curious paradox, he is a dramatist for listeners who are not habitual theatre-goers. A good claim could be made for Wagner as one of the most powerful of all influences upon modern drama. This is not evident in a country of such imperfect and discontinuous musical traditions as England; and even in musical countries it is obscured by the evident amateurishness of some aspects of Wagner's poetry. Moreover, the genuine qualities of Wagner's stagecraft are obscured by the determination with which he took upon himself the burden of every conceivable problem of scenery and production. In this he was probably wise; for his multiform talents did not all mature at the same rate, and he would have needed three hundred years of life before his *Allkunstwerk* could be equally mature in all its elements. Music was the art in which he attained full maturity. His poetry never became mature, though in *Tannhäuser*, and even in *Lohengrin*, it was far riper than his music had yet become. Through his mature music we can learn that he did indeed achieve an *Allkunstwerk*; that the imperfections of *The Ring*, *Tristan*, *Meistersinger*, and *Parsifal*, though they be as obvious as the imperfections of Shakespeare, are relatively as unimportant. The music is music-drama, the language is music interpretative of words, and the import of the words as interpreted by music is poetry of the highest order, whatever literary critics may be compelled to think of the words apart from the music.

The third act of *Parsifal* should be heard after the other two acts, and all three should be seen in action on the stage. Yet, even for listeners who have no such opportunity, the presentation of the third act in the concert-room has some advantages that can also be appreciated by listeners who know the whole work in its integrity. Brahms, who was by no means the anti-Wagnerian that most of his friends wished him to be, used to enjoy his Wagner operas one act at a time. One of my own most vivid experiences was that of hearing the second act of *Tristan* when I arrived in London too late for the first act. The unfatigued impression of it was enormously greater than any of my previous experiences. Of course it was essential to bring to the experience an intimate knowledge of the first act. Let us see now what we can make of the third act of *Parsifal* on the supposition that we have just heard and seen the other two acts and prefer now to listen to music with our eyes shut.

We have heard the wonderful prelude, which has given us all the themes of the Holy Grail; the curtain has risen upon a peaceful scene in the grounds of Monsalvat at dawn; and the good old

Brother Gurnemanz explains to two acolytes the story of the Grail
and the present tragic position of its guardian, Amfortas, whose
father, Titurel, still lives, but is kept alive only by the sight of the
Grail, which is unveiled in the communion service of its temple.
Long ago Klingsor had aspired to become a Knight of the Grail.
Unable to control his natural lusts, he made himself a eunuch and
offered himself to Titurel as a chaste candidate. Titurel rejected
him with scorn. In revenge he established himself in a wilderness
that lay in the path of pilgrims to Monsalvat, and turned this
wilderness into a magic garden full of temptations into which
many aspirants for the Brotherhood of the Grail fell. Amfortas
sallied forth to vanquish the sorcerer. He rashly took with him a
talisman of sanctity co-equal with the Grail itself: the Spear which
pierced the side of Christ crucified and drew the Blood that filled
the Cup. In Klingsor's enchanted garden Gurnemanz himself saw
the terrible fall of Amfortas, beguiled by a woman of appalling
beauty and caught in that unguarded moment by Klingsor, who
seized the holy Spear and wounded him with it. Gurnemanz
rescued him, but the Spear remained in Klingsor's unholy hands
and nothing can heal the wound of Amfortas.

Gurnemanz's tale is interrupted by the entry of Kundry, a wild
and distraught woman who brings with her a new balsam from
Arabia, with grimly small hope that it will be of any use for the
King's wound. The Brethren of the Grail always regard her with
suspicion, and she seems to hate them; yet, as Gurnemanz points
out, she is for ever busy on errands for them, and it is in her
absence that grave disasters befall them.

We see the suffering King Amfortas borne in a litter on his way
to bathe. He accepts the balsam with gratitude, and Gurnemanz
resumes his tale. In a vision Amfortas received a promise of salvation implied in the command to wait for the chosen one, the Pure
Fool who understands by pity. Gurnemanz's listeners, deeply
moved, softly repeat the well-remembered words of this promise,
but they are startled by a new and drastic interruption. In this
sanctuary, where all wild creatures are tame, somebody has shot a
swan. A trespasser, a youth strong and childlike, is brought in,
overpowered by four men. He is armed with a bow and arrows,
and sees no harm in hitting everything that flies. Gurnemanz soon
fills him with remorse for his thoughtless destruction of beautiful
life. He breaks his bow and arrows, and to all questions his only
answer is, 'I do not know'. He cannot remember his name, though
he has had many. All he can remember is that he has left his
mother, Herzeleide, and gone into the world with a bow and arrows
of his own making. Kundry suddenly supplements his story, and
tells us that he was born after the death of his father, Gamuret, in

battle. His foolish mother brought him up as a fool in order to
preserve him from a like fate. She adds that the boy became a
terror to robbers and giants. The strange youth asks in surprise:
'Who fears me?' She answers: 'The wicked.' 'Then were those
who fought me wicked? Who is good?' Gurnemanz says: 'Thy
mother, whom thou hast deserted and who is yearning and grieving
for thee.' To which Kundry roughly says: 'No more grief for her.
His mother is dead. I was riding by, and I saw her die. And she
sent her greeting to thee, thou fool.' Whereupon the strange
youth springs at her throat. Gurnemanz restrains him. The
strange youth trembles and is on the point of fainting. Kundry
brings him water and retires from the scene, over-mastered by the
dark power that enslaves her. Gurnemanz points out to him how
she returns good for ill. But we learn from her broken exclama-
tions that her own view is that she never does good. She longs for
peace and for sleep—but no, not sleep, anything rather than sleep!

Gurnemanz is forming the opinion that the strange youth is the
Pure Fool whose coming was promised. He goes with him to the
Hall of the Grail, in the hope that the promise may now be accomplished. Amfortas is borne on a litter to fulfil his holy office. The
voice of Titurel is heard from behind the altar, demanding the un-
veiling of the Grail. Amfortas protests passionately, for the performance of this office renews all the agonies of his wound. At
last voices from the heights of the dome remind him of the promised coming of the Pure Fool who understands by pity. Amfortas unveils the Grail and the solemnities proceed. At the end
it is evident that his wound has broken out again. Gurnemanz and
the youth are left alone, and Gurnemanz is disappointed to find
that the youth shows no understanding except a bewildered distress. He pushes the youth roughly out through a side-door,
advising him to leave swans alone and seek a goose for his gander-
ship. Nevertheless, a voice from above ends the act with an echo
of the promise.

In the second act we first see Klingsor in the topmost room of a
tower. He summons Kundry, who is in his power because he is
the only man who has not yielded to her. A rash boast, for she is
able to taunt him with the shameful secret of his power. She, the
Rose of Hell, had (as we learn later) seen Christ bearing His Cross
and had laughed. His gaze had fallen upon her, and she was doomed
to tarry till He should come again. Now she must deal with the
most dangerous of all Klingsor's enemies, as she had already dealt
with Amfortas. From his tower Klingsor sees the youth fighting
his way into the garden through all the opposition the recreant
knights can give. The scene changes, and we see the youth beset
by a crowd of enchantresses in flower-like guise. He is quite ready

to play with them, if only they will give him room and not crowd round him so closely. Suddenly he hears an over-mastering voice calling him by his forgotten name, Parsifal. The *Blumenmädchen* are dismissed by a mightier enchantress. Kundry appears in radiant beauty and holds him spellbound with talk of his mother, Herzeleide. At last she says that his dying mother sent him through her a kiss. At the kiss Parsifal starts up, enlightened by pity and terror, crying: 'Amfortas, the wound!' The prophecy is fulfilled. He knows all, and Kundry's most agonized efforts can force from him only the promise that he was sent for her salvation also, but by means far other than those she asks. Her only remaining power is to lay upon him a curse which shall make his return to the suffering Amfortas a long wandering through devious ways. Klingsor appears, imagining himself once more triumphant, and hurls the sacred Spear at Parsifal. Parsifal grasps the Spear and makes with it the sign of the Cross; whereupon Klingsor's castle crashes into ruin and all the flowers wither. Parsifal departs, telling Kundry that she knows where she will find him again.

The third act begins with a mysterious quiet prelude on themes which we have not heard before. It gives an impression of sorrow—

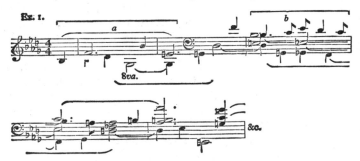

and of wandering footsteps that must often be retraced in order to find the right path.

A short crescendo incidentally reminds us of the Dresden Amen and leads to Kundry's wildest outcry, accompanied by three notes that suffice to remind us of fig. (*c*) of the Grail-theme that has become associated with the holy Spear.

Ex. 3.

continued in Ex. 6.

(For convenience I append the Dresden Amen and the Grail-theme in their original forms.)

Ex. 4.

Ex. 5.

A vigorous theme now pursues its way through all obstacles.

Ex. 6.

(In it we recognize a transformation of the theme that promised the coming of the Pure Fool.)

Ex. 7.

Durch Mit - leid   wis-send,   der   rei - ne   Tor;

The climax subsides, and a plaintive chromatic wailing is heard—

Ex. 8.

which had once been a lively feature of the whirling seductive dance of the *Blumenmädchen* in Klingsor's garden. The curtain rises upon a lovely forest-scene at the edge of the Grail-precincts, profuse with springtide flowers far lovelier and more life-enhancing than the tropical glories of Klingsor's garden. Some creature concealed in the bushes is moaning.

Ex. 9.

From Ex. 9 we know that it is Kundry; and while we are reminded of Klingsor—

Ex. 10.   &c.

the door of a hut opens and Gurnemanz, now much aged and retired as a hermit, comes out to see what this moaning may be, more piteous than the plaint of any stricken hare, and most unlikely on this holiest of days (themes anticipating Exx. 22 and 16). He finds Kundry collapsed and unconscious in a thicket of brambles. He revives her with difficulty. At last she awakens with a wild cry. Yet there is no wildness left in her. She is in the robe of a penitent, her face is pale, and after gazing long at Gurnemanz she rises, sets in order her hair, and moves as if to go to work like a serving-maid. Gurnemanz asks in surprise if she has no word to say to him. At last, after a long effort, she is able to say: 'Dienen, dienen.' Gurnemanz shakes his head. Service will give her no trouble. There are no more errands. We seek our simples and herbs for ourselves, learning from the beasts of the forest. Kundry sees the hut and goes into it, as if she knew her duty. Gurnemanz watches her in wonder. Is this the effect of Good Friday? And has Heaven allowed him to revive her to-day for her salvation? Kundry, coming out of the hut with a water-jug, goes with it to the well. She points out to Gurnemanz an approaching stranger.

Ex. 11.

He is in black armour with closed visor. Bearing a lowered spear, he enters slowly with drooping head. He seats himself on a little knoll by the spring. Gurnemanz, watching him in astonishment, greets him and asks him if he has lost his way. He gently shakes his head and merely nods when Gurnemanz asks him if he has no greeting. 'If thou art vowed to silence, I am vowed to tell thee what is fit. This is a holy place, where no man comes armed with closed helmet and shield and spear, least of all to-day. Do you not know what holy day this is? No? What heathen company have you been keeping, that you do not know that this is the holiest Good Friday morning? Down with those weapons! Vex not the Lord Who to-day weaponless gave His holy Blood as atonement for the sinful world.'

The knight thrusts the holy Spear into the ground before him, lays his shield and his own spear down, opens and takes off his helmet and puts it with the other weapons, and then kneels in silent prayer. Gurnemanz watches him with astonishment and emotion, and calls to Kundry, saying: 'Do you recognize him? This is he who killed the swan. This is the Fool whom I angrily dismissed. The Spear, I know it. Oh that I should awaken to see this holiest of days!'

Ex. 12.

Kundry turns away her face, overcome with the sorrow of penitence.

Ex. 13.

Parsifal slowly rises from his prayer, recognizes Gurnemanz and greets him. In his long wanderings the beardless youth has grown into a Christlike man. He tells how he has trodden the path of error and suffering (Ex. 2). He now recognizes the murmur of this forest and the greeting of this good old man, yet all seems altered. Is he still at loss? 'Whom are you seeking?' asks Gurnemanz. Parsifal replies that he is seeking one whose deep woe he once saw in foolish wonder—

Ex. 14.

and for whose healing he deems himself ordained. But a curse has driven him in pathless wanderings, and he has had to fight his way, defending the Spear itself from attack, for he dared not use it as a

weapon; undefiled, he has carried it and brought it here, the holy
Spear of the Grail. When Gurnemanz has mastered his emotion
at this fulfilment of the vision of Titurel—

Ex. 15.

he assures Parsifal that, whatever curse kept him from his goal, its
power has ceased. This is indeed the region of the Grail, whose
Knighthood awaits Parsifal and is in dire need of the healing that
he brings. Since Parsifal has left them, Amfortas has wished for
nothing but death—

Ex. 16.

and refused to perform his office. Now at last Titurel, deprived of
the sight of the Grail that gave him life, has died, like all mortal
men.

Parsifal breaks out in an agony of remorse at his own folly that
has caused all this woe. He is on the point of fainting. Kundry
hastily fetches a bowl of water. As she returns we hear a pathetic
echo of the last plea of her temptation of Parsifal: 'Nur eine
Stunde dein.'

Ex. 17.

Gurnemanz gently intervenes, for the Holy Well itself must be the
pilgrim's bath.

Ex. 18.

He has a high task to-day before him.

Kundry and Gurnemanz lead Parsifal to the edge of the spring.
They remove his breastplate and greaves. Parsifal asks: 'Shall I be
led to Amfortas to-day?' Gurnemanz answers that the Hall of the
Grail awaits them.

Ex. 19.

To-day is the funeral of Titurel, and Amfortas has promised as a last token of repentance to unveil the Grail. Parsifal, now in his white robe an unmistakable type of Christ, gazes on Kundry as, like the Magdalene, she washes his feet. He says to her: as she has washed his feet, so let his friend now besprinkle his head. Gurnemanz, scooping with his hand water from the spring, performs the rite; and Kundry completes the history of the Magdalene by producing a vessel of precious ointment which she pours over Parsifal's feet and then dries with her hair. Parsifal takes the vessel gently from her and hands it to Gurnemanz that the friend of Titurel may anoint his head as King.

With this ceremony the well-known concert-room excerpt known as the Good-Friday music begins. As a beautiful piece of orchestral colour I had often enjoyed it in the concert-room, like the kind of 'sugar piled upon honey' that Lamb disenjoyed as his only idea of music; and I was interested to find, when I heard it in its proper context at Bayreuth, that I had no recollection of it whatever. In the early days of modern Homeric criticism, one Lachmann discovered that the *Iliad* of Homer was cleverly put together from a number of old ballads or lays. The difficulty about Lachmann's lays was that, though the lays of this person and that person all had excellent beginnings, they all petered out vaguely. More recent criticism has found precisely the same phenomenon in the novels of Dickens and of every writer of fiction sufficiently voluminous to be driven to introduce characters and groups of persons with a separate exposition. With a great epic or a great novel these separate expositions can always be prised out of the total mass by misplaced ingenuity; but the naïve reader or listener is the better critic in that he does not notice this possibility. With Wagner the popularity of concert extracts with (or without) plausible beginnings has efficiently destroyed all standards of musical finality and form. The Good-Friday music can be shut off somehow, as you can switch off your wireless.

Gurnemanz solemnly anoints Parsifal as King. Parsifal fulfils his first office by baptizing the kneeling Kundry.

Ex. 20.

&c.

Her age-long curse is over. Her laughter at the suffering Christ had always overcome her again and again whenever a sinner fell into her power, but now at last she can weep, and she is shaken with the peaceful tears of her penitence (Ex. 13).

Parsifal admires the lovely springtime flowers around him, so different from the tropical glories of Klingsor's garden.

Ex. 21.

Gurnemanz says that this flowering is the magic of Good Friday. Parsifal is astonished that on this day of highest agony all that breathes should not mourn and sorrow. Gurnemanz says: 'You see, that is not so.' All creation blossoms, watered by the sinners' tears. Unable to see Christ Himself on the Cross, it looks up to redeemed mankind.

Ex. 22.

At last Kundry raises her head and gazes in grave longing up to Parsifal. He, remembering the mocking flowers of Klingsor's garden, recognizes that they too may look for redemption. Kundry weeps, and the landscape smiles. He kisses her on the brow with the kiss of peace. The bells of the temple peal in the distance.

Ex. 23.

Bells.   Orchestral version.

It is midday. Gurnemanz and Kundry array Parsifal in the mantle of a Knight of the Grail. Parsifal grasps the holy Spear and follows Gurnemanz with Kundry. We approach the Hall of the Grail with dark harmonies of tremendous solemnity. First they recall the sorrow of Herzeleide, Parsifal's mother, as related to him by Kundry. Then they merge into the funeral of Titurel, amid the thunderous tolling of bells.

Within the Hall, from one side a procession bears the body of Titurel in his coffin. From the other side a procession carries Amfortas on his sick-bed with the veiled Shrine of the Grail. The procession of Amfortas asks the other procession what it is that they are bringing. They answer that their burden is the hero to whom God entrusted a holy power.

FIRST PROCESSION: Who has slain him who was thus protected by God?

SECOND PROCESSION: He was felled by the burden of age, since he could no more behold the Grail.

I: Who barred him from seeing the grace of the Grail?

II: He whom you are bearing, its sinful warden.

I: We bring him to-day, for once more he will do his office for the last time!

BOTH PROCESSIONS: Alas, for the last time!

Amfortas wearily raises himself. He would rather receive death from them as the lightest atonement for his sin. The coffin is opened; and at the sight of Titurel's corpse all cry out with grief. Amfortas raises himself upright and addresses the corpse. He implores his father, most blessed and purest of heroes, to whom angels had spoken, and to whom he who alone wished to die had given death. He beseeches him who is now beholding the Redeemer Himself in divine glory, to beg that the holy Blood which gives new life to the Brethren shall at last give death to the sufferer.

The Knights press around Amfortas, bidding him uncover the Grail. In a fury of despair Amfortas leaps from his bed, tears open his robe, and bids them plunge their swords into his wound. Let them kill the sinner with his pain, and the Grail will shine by itself.

Meanwhile, Parsifal has entered unnoticed among the Knights. He comes forward and touches the wound of Amfortas with the holy Spear. Gurnemanz supports the enraptured Amfortas, whose wound is healed. He is now simply a Knight of the Grail. Blessed from henceforth are his past sufferings, which gave the highest power of pity and pure knowledge to the timid Fool. From the point of the holy Spear, which has healed Amfortas's wound, there is a miraculous flow of Blood, which aspires to rejoin its origin in the Holy Grail. The Grail shall never be closed again. Uncover the Grail; open the Shrine!

Parsifal fulfils his office. The choir sings 'Salvation to the Saviour!' The White Dove descends and hovers over Parsifal's head. For Kundry this is the second coming of Christ, and she is released from the bondage of earthly life.

Ex. 24.

RETROSPECT AND CORRIGENDA

The lacunae in these volumes are vast, obvious, and casual. In Vol. II, in the Preface I have explained those that result from general and local conditions; and I have now to fill up merely capricious gaps by mentioning some of the missing works.

The greatest and most obvious defect is in the representation of modern music. I have explained the cause of this in the Preface to Vol. II, and need only repeat here that I am not to blame for not producing things hopelessly beyond local opportunities.

As to the classics, the most apparent lacuna is Handel, who is represented only by *Israel in Egypt*, and by one not very well-known concerto. In my analysis I have referred to the 'de-Bestification' of Handel's organ concertos as a task second in difficulty only to that imposed on us by Handel's inveterate habit of not writing his music down. On the other side of the late W. T. Best yawns the deep sea of the still later Chrysander and his surviving hosts of *Musikgelehrte*. In my *Companion to the Art of Fugue* I have pointed out how impossible it is for a rapid writer not to let such figures as ♩. ♫. ♩ degenerate into every permutation and combination of ♩ ♫. ♩♩. ♫ ♩ and ♩ ♫ ♩. On the maintenance of these subtle distinctions the *Musikgelehrte* are all Mumpsimites[1] to a man. But they are not less zealous in putting into the solo and orchestral parts of Handel's works their own cadenzas and conjectures, together with every record of what any eighteenth-century singing-master may have taught to any singer within living memory of Handel. The fact is that every self-respecting conductor wants to rewrite Handel; or rather, to write him out completely in the first place, and, in the second place, to adapt him to the severely restricted conditions of the modern orchestra. For the paradox of Handel's orchestration is that while neither it nor any other music, not even the *Requiem* of Berlioz nor the symphonies of Mahler, was ever designed for performance on the scale of our Crystal Palace Handel Festivals, it nevertheless presupposes quite as many oboes and bassoons as strings; and at present the proper conditions for its performance simply do not exist. Various great conductors have their ways of tackling Handel: my own conceit enables me to agree with them

---

[1] This word is not in *O.E.D.*, nor in its Supplement. It refers to the scrupulous monk, mentioned in one of Sir Walter Scott's introductions, who persisted in reading *mumpsimus* for *sumpsimus*.

only as the missionary agreed with his fellow-workers of another denomination: 'we both serve the same Master, you in your way and I in His.'

Bach is easier: his works are technically more difficult and therefore present problems which the performers learn on the spot; and, except for the continuo, they are completely written out. The continuo itself is an ideal method of training students in harmony. The only thing that has prevented me from doing more Bach at the Reid Concerts is that his orchestra contributes little to the heartbreaking task of improving the musical climate of Edinburgh.

Mozart is not badly represented in these essays. The 'Prague' Symphony has arrived too late for inclusion; and the 'Paris' Symphony, a very important historic document, I have just been able to produce in the present volume, where with Gluck and C. P. E. Bach it completes the picture of the transition from the continuo to the self-supporting orchestra. It was a shock to me to realize that the most famous (and justly famous) of all Mozart's pianoforte concertos, the D minor, is missing. We have played it several times, but on Sundays. The 'Coronation' Concerto in D major we have not done; that splendid comedy the F major (Köchel 459) has occurred too late; so has the larger B flat major (K. 456) with its wonderful G minor variations; and there are at least four other pianoforte concertos which I intend to produce as opportunity arises. At Sunday concerts we have produced the concerto for two pianofortes; and some day we may find it amusing to produce the opusculum for three, perhaps on an occasion when we are producing the triple concertos of Bach. It is difficult to get together three harpsichords, ancient or modern, that will match, and I have no more scruple than Philipp Emanuel Bach had in using the pianoforte for Bach and Handel, so long as the instrument is under more intelligent control than that of a 'pianistic' player of the Tschopsztiksy school.

Of Mozart's violin concertos the two represented here are the perfect examples. There are three[1] earlier ones; and a slightly later one in D major, discovered in this century and certainly genuine though the solo part has been tampered with. By a perversity not unusual in the case of Mozart, the violin concerto that is most often played is a voluminous work in E flat, welcome to violinists because its technique is more advanced than that of the other concertos, but obviously in so shocking a mess as to scoring and details that it cannot possibly be genuine as it stands. Perhaps a genuine work might assume such a shape, if an unmusicianly enthusiast had before him the solo part with its outline of the

[1] Four, since the recent discovery of a sketchy specimen of his prodigious childhood.

tuttis, and tried to make a full score from its data. At present the work looks as if the composition were all wrong (as is demonstrably the case with the Concertante for four wind instruments and orchestra). But incompetent or spurious accompaniments have an astonishing power to obliterate masterly form. Among Mozart's ripest and wittiest works is a set of Divertimenti for two clarinets and bassoon which, until early in this century, were, in the most accurate sense of the term, obliterated by spurious parts for a pair of horns. I have not yet investigated the E flat violin concerto closely enough to see whether it presents a case for restoration. At present it does not make sense or grammar. The Concertante for four wind instruments, on the other hand, presents no case for restoration. In the sense that 'the soul is either blue or not blue', it can be construed; but the man who wrote it could not compose. He could not, for instance, have been Pleyel, who wrote concertantes galore, but who was a pupil of Haydn.

The Concertante Symphony (a curious but authentic title) for violin and viola is an important early work which we have played several times. My excellent first horn, Mr. Walter Worsley, has produced for us Mozart's four horn concertos in all their bubbling humour. The analysis of them yields amusing points, but nothing quite so funny as the scurrilous remarks in Mozart's autographs. And these would distract attention from the music.

Mozart's flute music with orchestra is represented completely in these essays. This we owe to the kindness of that great flautist, my lamented friend Louis Fleury, who came to our aid in the earliest days of the Reid Orchestra and joyfully helped us to commemorate the founder of the Reid Chair on or about his birthday, February 13, by producing his genuine flute sonatas, instead of the traditional pot-pourri, heavily upholstered in orchestration of the Mahogany Age that passed for 'the Reid Music' from the 'sixties onwards. Fleury created quite a vogue for General Reid's sonatas in Paris.

In the wildly improbable event of any demand arising for more of these essays, I may as well say that I do not propose to collect any more analyses of Mozart's and Haydn's instrumental works in future volumes. Nothing short of précis-writing can reveal the constant and vital differences between each work. And it may be news to some readers that I find précis-writing of Haydn and Mozart far too difficult for any but the most advanced of my students; especially if they have come to the University primed with traditional views of musical form. These are about as useful as bird's-eye views of architecture; and half the energy of three or four years of intensive training is spent in getting the Bird's Eye into human pedestrian focus.

Something has been said in these essays about the infuriating conditions for producing Haydn's symphonies. By great good fortune Haydn himself looked after the publication of his string quartets; with the result that, while much remains to be discovered, such as Miss Marion Scott's first-rate historical document, Haydn's actual first quartet, earlier than Op. 1, No. 1, all such discoveries are certain to be of historic rather than artistic importance. Haydn himself wished to ignore everything earlier than his set of six quartets known as Op. 9. From that point onwards his art, as shown by the quartets, lives by its absolute values, and makes enormous progress from perfection within primitive conditions to perfection on higher and higher planes. Now the symphonies, acknowledged as such, begin at a higher level than the quartets of Opp. 1 and 2. (The line between string quartet and string orchestra is at first obscure, and wind parts have been discovered for some of the early 'quartets'.) But the first fifty symphonies do not advance to the level of the best quartets in Op. 9; and, as I have reiterated elsewhere, a case might be argued for the proposition that Haydn's famous opportunities for experimenting with the orchestra at Esterhaz did him as much harm as good. At all events, the experimental elements in the first fifty symphonies consist in outbreaks of fantastic virtuosity for individual players, who, whether residents or visitors, were doubtless able to do justice to them. But meanwhile the general orchestral organization made no appreciable progress. The learned editor of the fourth volume does not comfort me for the delay in its appearance by his remarks about the impossibility of reproducing the living features of Haydn's handwriting by any process short of facsimile. The remarks are charmingly expressed, but they will apply to any handwriting by any lively person. I saw the whole volume in proof on Mandyczewski's table in 1928. A delay of six years in publishing does not seem adequately excused by the discovery that one symphony is five years earlier than Mandyczewski supposed, and that here and there Haydn wrote ♩ ♪♪♪ in the score where the parts read ♫ ♫ ♫ . Such matters can be treated, as was the custom of the best nineteenth-century scholars, in a later volume of *Revisionsberichte*. Moreover, I confess to an attitude which the modern *Musikgelehrte* may perhaps think snobbish, but which would certainly advance or restore the standard of musical scholarship if it were more often adopted. I am prepared to appreciate the importance of the erratum 'for *buz'd* read *buzz'd*' if the work concerned is *Paradise Lost*, but if it occurs only in Johnson's translation of Lobo's *Travels in Abyssinia* I shall not even trouble to see if I have quoted that title correctly.

Meanwhile, not being an expert collector, I cannot pick up printed full scores of more than twelve of the forty-two most epoch-making symphonies in the history of music; those in which Haydn matured his style after leaving Esterhaz and before crowning his work with the twelve London symphonies. On the back of the fourth volume of the critical edition of Haydn's symphonies the contents of the whole first series of the *Denkmäler Deutscher Tonkunst* are advertised. Far be it from me to deny that there are good things galore in those sixty-five volumes. But in comparison with the missing middle Haydn symphonies their catalogue reads like the list Stevenson drew up of the books a certain firm of publishers triumphantly issued as compared with the list of what they rejected. *Jones's Latin Irregular Verbs*; *Robinson's Stately Homes of Salop*, &c., &c., as against the rejected comedy *April Rain*, the Biblical tragedy of *David and Bathsheba*, and an autobiography up to the production of *King John*—by William Shakespeare; five books of an unfinished novel, *Solomon Crabbe*, by Henry Fielding, &c.

Beethoven's orchestral music is almost completely represented in these essays. The second concerto (really the first) in B flat is missing. A few words here will prevent the omission from being a serious lacuna. The first movement is full of jolly early Beethoven diversions, but is far more scattered than even the first movement of the C major concerto. The most amusing thing about it is that, as with the C major concerto, Beethoven revived his interest in the work later on and wrote a big cadenza for it. But whereas the best of the three cadenzas for the first movement of the C major concerto is a magnificent thing which raises the status of the whole work, this cadenza to the B flat concerto is one of the most amusing exhibitions of temper that any artist or animal ever showed in the first or last stages of casting a skin. Brahms's grafting of his latest ideas on to the stock of his early B major trio shows, as Röntgen always complained, a certain unfriendliness at the moments when the old composer grabs the young one by the scruff of his neck and kicks ripe wisdom into him; but it shows nothing like the temper of the improvisatorial-inquisitorial, valedictory-maledictory fugato in which Beethoven storms for several pages over the whole newly extended compass of his pianoforte on a subject and counter-subject as loosely connected with the rest of the movement as all its themes and developments are connected with each other. The slow movement and rondo are masterpieces; and it is a mere accident that I have not yet produced the whole concerto at the Reid Concerts. The rondo is Beethoven's second finale; he wrote an earlier one which appeared posthumously and would be worth playing as a separate piece, if the pianoforte part had not unfortunately been completed by Czerny in his most musical-box style.

The first movements of two juvenile concertos exist, but my programmes are concerned only with absolute musical values. Slightness and inequalities do not matter; but I have no use for *merely* historical music, though the chamber music of Edinburgh University is produced under the title of the Historical Concerts. I have not had an opportunity of producing the *Egmont* music, which in Germany keeps what is by no means Goethe's best play alive upon the stage. The difficulties of producing the music in the concert-room can be surmounted only by some form of recitation. This would certainly be worth while. Of *Die Ruinen von Athen* the overture is an amusing piece of genuine 'light music' for which I may some day find room; the solemn March in E flat, with or without chorus, is noble; the chorus of Dervishes is first-rate; and the famous Turkish March is neither better nor worse than its reputation. Altogether this *pièce d'occasion* does not contain enough good fragments to group together in a satisfactory way. Of *König Stephan* I intend to produce neither the overture nor any of the rest. The eminent critic Rochlitz, like some of Beethoven's best friends, was distressed at the master's small output in the year 1812, and at its increasingly theatrical style. In fact, Beethoven's energy was at this period sadly drained by lawsuits, chiefly about the guardianship of his scapegrace nephew; and the theatricality of *Die Ruinen von Athen* and *König Stephan* was hardly out of place in the theatre. Nevertheless Beethoven was irritated by Rochlitz's criticisms; though he thought far worse of these works than the elegant Rochlitz ventured to suggest. The late Dr. Prieger, of Bonn, showed me a bound volume of Rochlitz's musical journal with Beethoven's furious notes. In these outspoken days it may be permissible to convey the substance of Beethoven's remarks by summing it up as a comparison between his waste products and Rochlitz's highest thoughts, to the disadvantage of the latter.

The early ballet *Die Geschöpfe des Prometheus* presents a rather intriguing problem to the designer of classical programmes. The editors of the *Gesammtausgabe* of Beethoven's works were such absolute musicians that they removed almost all such vulgarities as stage-directions and dialogue from most of the theatre-music of Mozart and Beethoven. Much of the *Prometheus* music is broken up by pauses in a manner entirely pointless without the choreography; and large tracts of the music are monotonously frivolous. But the overture is excellent early Beethoven, beginning with a stroke of genius and leading to quite a good thunderstorm on the stage. In all there is something like an hour and a half of orchestral music in the work. The high lights are a piece with a solo violoncello and a harp, doubtless representing how the lyre and voice of Prometheus gave life to his clay images; and the finale, a rondo on the theme which afterwards became glorified in the Variations, Op. 35, and in the finale of the 'Eroica' Symphony. The famous 'Battle' Symphony (*Wellington's Sieg oder die Schlacht bei Vittoria*) I shall neither produce nor describe here. A description of it would be amusing; but the perky-precious reaction against Beethoven is too recent for fun at Beethoven's expense to be permissible now.

My conscience is clear as to the representation of Schubert's orchestral music. In the case of Schumann, the omission of the C major Symphony is a serious lacuna; but, by way of compensation, in the present volume I have been able to produce the *Overture, Scherzo, and Finale* which sheer perversity induced Schumann to deprive of its original title of *Sinfonietta*. We have also successfully produced the Concerto for four horns, an interesting though nearly impossible work, of which my analysis has been crowded out.

Brahms is completely represented, except for some of the choral works. Some day I hope to deal with certain misunderstood aspects of his style. At present things like the middle 4/4 section of the 'Tragic' Overture, and the ruminating triplet theme in the finale of the Second Symphony (see Vol. I, p. 105, Ex. 26) are as completely beyond the comprehension of the average concert-goer as the style of Bach was beyond John Hullah, who, in the 'sixties or 'seventies, was the first person to say that 'Bach is so SATISFACTORY', but who denied him all intention or capacity of expression beyond such as we can ascribe to the Great Pyramid. A supplementary note on the 'Tragic' Overture in the present volume attempts to discuss this matter, or at least to indicate its existence (Essay CCXXXIX).

It only remains for me to deal with Wagner. I claim for these programmes that they represent fairly exactly so much of Wagner's mature work as can be decently produced in the concert-room at all. Time is running short, space is exhausted; your patience, dear reader, does not matter so much, because you have been emphatically warned that these volumes are intended to be read skippingly; but *my* patience is now completely exhausted and I must beg leave to hasten this conclusion by pontificating. Perhaps it has escaped your notice that hitherto I have always tried to prove my points; and, as Dr. Johnson said in the most pathetic of all his recorded utterances, 'Sir I consider myself a very polite man'. But now, as Dr. Johnson said on another occasion, taking the words out of his disputant's mouth, 'we are to be as rude as we please'. I don't ask for belief: but it will save time if I pontificate that anybody who turns up his nose at the *Kaisermarsch* will just have to keep it turned up, as is the fate of nurse-scared children who make faces when the wind changes. The merits of the *Kaisermarsch* are not political affairs. Either you can recognize grand style and grand composition or you can't. I have attempted to analyse the *Kaisermarsch* in this volume, and have taken the opportunity of dealing faithfully with the question of Wagnerian excerpts.

For the rest, let us never forget that these volumes are a collection of occasional notes, produced mainly over a period of twenty-one years and including material already written in 1902. It would be a mistake to try to give them more coherent form. The collection has, in fact, a form that arises naturally from its origin, and which secures an immunity from criticisms that would be fatal to a work with more serious pretensions. Yet the whole collection has been noticed to present the appearance of a solid body of consistent musical doctrine; and, if I had an uneasy conscience as to the duty of changing one's opinions as one changes one's linen, I should have been worried by the fact that the opinions I expressed in 1902 were essentially the same as those I wish to express in 1938. Part of this immutability comes from my subject-matter. I have never been concerned with musical fashions; and my master, Parry, taught me to study the classics of music from point to point according to the course of each individual work, instead of setting up classical forms *a priori* and treating the individual work as if it were compelled to fit the forms. Parry's method, being thus elastic, cannot change; and a series of essays all written according to this method can show no progress, except in the range of its subjects. That range, as I am always pointing out, has been limited for me, by no means by my taste but by the practical restrictions on the repertoire of an orchestra limited to six hours' practice a week and seldom able to afford instruments that Brahms would have regarded as extras. Obviously in such circumstances my reviews of modern music must be few, and irreducible to a coherent scheme. If my orchestra had had daily practice and support for some such series as the London Promenade Concerts, these volumes would have represented my views on modern music with a much less reactionary appearance. On this matter I think the time now ripe for me to divulge a piece of musical history.

In 1902, when the second edition of Grove's *Dictionary* was in progress, I was invited to write an article on Richard Strauss. I was gratified by the invitation, and had every intention of complying with the editor's request. I understood that he would prefer my detached view to that of a partisan who was likely to see little merit in any other music. On the other hand, he could trust me not to be shocked out of all sense of proportion by unorthodoxies in Strauss's technique. Unfortunately I was in Berlin at the time; and there both the Straussians and the anti-Straussians were actively making what capital they could by sniggering over minor details in Strauss's subject-matter which persons unacquainted with French literature were pleased to call Rabelaisian, and which canny Scots would call 'sculduddery'. These things were neither here nor there. I was then, and still am, adequately impressed with Strauss's immense powers of composition; moments of high pathos, such as were to culminate later in the recognition of Orestes by Electra, moved me profoundly; I rather enjoyed the more sensational and horrific elements of his style; and the only thing that thoroughly repelled me was his frequent fits of prettiness, in which he seemed to treat beauty with a parodistic patronage which I thought insulting. I felt then much as I feel now: that it was little use to be *rein musikalisch* unless one was thoroughly *rein* to begin with; and some of the Straussian beauty seemed to me as ineligible for great music as Klingsor was for the Brotherhood of the Grail. Of the 'sculduddery' I also thought then as I think now: it reminded me of a boy showing a younger boy life in a railway refreshment room by ordering a brandy-and-soda, into which he solemnly dropped three lumps of sugar.

Such were my views in 1902; neither then nor now would they have prevented me from contributing to Grove's *Dictionary* an article on Strauss which Grove himself would have approved. I should have explained to the best of my ability the enormous efficiency of Strauss's mastery, his command of movement in free composition, and, had *Elektra* by then appeared, his musical stage-craft and capacity to inspire the actors of his music-dramas. To matters of taste I should have referred as to things about which dispute is proverbially unprofitable. Unfortunately, in 1902 the habit of scandal-mongering in musical criticism was not yet obsolete. Even then this difficulty could have been tackled by a man of the world with a light touch. I felt that I had neither the lightness of touch nor the knowledge of the world; and I accordingly wrote to the editor of the second edition of Grove and told him that any contribution from me on the subject would be far too heavy-handed. When the new edition appeared I bitterly regretted my withdrawal, and wondered how I had ever been gulled by charm of manner into taking the editor for a man of the world. He wrote the article himself and produced one of the most notorious and ill-timed outpourings of vituperation in the whole history of criticism. Much of the article was judicious enough in a patronizing way, but it descended to an implication of 'pornography' (which is a much worse word than 'sculduddery') and angrily accused Strauss of 'impertinence', besides constantly implying that the whole of Strauss's intentions were fraudulent. It is not too much to say that that article sufficed to ruin the reputation of the second edition of Grove's *Dictionary*. The music of Richard

Strauss may have stood for everything that Sir George Grove would have hated if he had known it; but everybody who knew his conception of his duties as editor felt that this article must have made him turn in his grave. In the light of the event, I should have been far wiser to have contributed my own fumbling efforts. If I had had the slightest idea that the editor would have taken the line he did, I would have risked any number of tactless blunders of my own.

But the reason why Strauss appears only twice in these volumes is not a matter of taste. It is the mere result of the fact that he regards as the normal orchestra three of each wind instrument instead of two. Some modern composers—Bax, for instance—will describe their own scores as written for a chamber orchestra unless they are using three or four of each wind instrument. Until the Reid Orchestra is better supported, such luxuries can seldom appear in my programmes; and the Edinburgh public will forgive me for pointing out that it is rather more proud than ashamed of its dislike of modern music. By way of compensation, we have covered an unusually wide range of classical music, and the pieces which we have performed oftenest have not been those that are most hackneyed elsewhere; nor have we played anything so often that it has become stale to us.

Our Sunday concerts, for which no analytical programmes are issued, have included much that we have not produced at a Reid Concert. Hence several lacunae, of which the most astonishing is that there is no analysis of the most famous, the most perfect, and, if so disputable a term be worth risking, the greatest of all Mozart's concertos: the D minor, Köchel No. 466. Obviously no review of Mozart's concertos could be regarded as complete if it omitted the most important of all; but these volumes cannot pretend to give a complete view of any particular set of classics. I could hardly have gone to press with a collection which, containing as much as it does, should omit any one of the nine symphonies of Beethoven; but even with these the essays are manifestly too unequal in scale to be regarded as much more than a chance collection of *obiter dicta.*

The reception given by the Press to these volumes has far exceeded my wildest expectations. Without exception, those critics who have pointed out my mistakes have reserved their strictures to the end of reviews that strike a note of generous appreciation. My errors are numerous, and nothing would have been easier than for a critic to draw up a list of them in a form calculated to expose me as a humbug. I owe it to the critics, and to the general public, to correct these errors, and I beg individual critics to forgive me for shirking the complicated task of distinguishing to which of them I owe particular corrections. One quality I may claim to share with Dr. Johnson, and that is a complete lack of method and a shameless and indolent reliance upon a well-stocked memory. If and when these volumes, or any parts of them, are reprinted, many corrections will be incorporated in the text, but no attempt will be made to turn my armchair garrulity into a serious work of reference. My only claim to solidity is in respect of purely musical analysis; and here I am far too slippery a customer to reward criticism, my fundamental proposition being that most of the orthodox terms and methods of musical analysis are rubbish, so that I am as free in my terminology as Humpty Dumpty, while my lacunae are self-confessed. One very important musical matter which I despair of clearing up is the innumerable errors in the musical examples. It is difficult to discriminate between legitimate sketchiness, such as a generalized form for a theme that recurs in several versions (with the consequent omission of slurs and other marks of expression), and real slips of memory and of the pen. But if ever another edition of this collection is required I will try to secure some Hercules to wash out the Augean stables of my quotations.

As to dates and biographical details, I owe the debt of gratitude we all owe to the authors of that most emancipating intellectual maxim of modern times, viz. *History is what you remember.* Their cardinal date of 1066 is the only one that is indelibly graven on the tablets of my mind, and I often feel vague as to what event it commemorates. I only know that it is too early for the birth of Bach. In writing my essays I have consulted, when time and opportunity permitted, the nearest available references, which have usually been the second edition of Grove and my own articles in the *Encyclopædia Britannica.* However, now for an effort to correct some errors that have been pointed out by my generous and tolerant critics.

Of these, the grossest are certain statements about Brahms's *Requiem* and Debussy's *Damoiselle Élue.* Brahms's *Requiem* was not written in commemoration of the fallen in the Franco-Prussian War; and its soprano solo commemorated his mother, not his step-mother. Debussy did not submit *La Damoiselle Élue* for the *Prix de Rome.*

Misprints (which, I flatter myself, I could correct more easily if the Oxford University Press committed more of them) have, for the most part, been corrected in second impressions. Of my own mistakes I can find nothing important in Vol. I. On page 101 the Allegretto of Brahms's Second Symphony is said to have four horns: it has only three. This is the kind of thing the composer himself may or may not discover after he has finished his score.

Page 161:—the fanfares in the Allegretto of the 'Military' Symphony may possibly have some connexion with the fact that Haydn did actually write a set for an English regiment while he was in London.

The footnote on page 214 raises a question slightly more complex than I thought at the time of writing. The fact is that the only possible range of tempo for Andante con moto ⅜ is precisely the same as that for Allegro moderato ¾, beat for beat. Accordingly, most conductors assume that the andante beats must at all costs be decidedly slower than those of the first movement. This is one of those scruples which, cogent as articles of *a priori* faith, absolutely vanish in real life. No two symphonic movements are more perfectly contrasted than the Allegro and Andante of the 'Unfinished' Symphony, and the contrast would not be impaired if the tempi were exactly equal, or even if the Allegro were broadened, and the con moto of the Andante exaggerated till it were actually the faster of the two movements.

On page 220 acknowledgement should be made to Prout for his comment on Mendelssohn's wisdom in omitting oboes from the repeated chords at the beginning of Mendelssohn's 'Italian' Symphony. Prout is less happy in remarking that Mendelssohn's effect is better than that of Beethoven in the Allegretto of his Eighth Symphony; there is nothing in common between the passages but their appearance on paper. Beethoven's is a deliberate 'tick-tick-tick', first drafted by him as a canon on Maelzel's metronome. Mendelssohn's is the ἀνήριθμον γέλασμα of the sea, a *tour de force* of tonguing for the wood-wind.

The inequalities in the analyses of the Beethoven symphonies are beyond remedy, nor do I wish to deprive students of the opportunity of working out for themselves what is needed to make the analyses as complete as my précis of the Ninth Symphony.

Volume II

The mistakes in Vol. II are more numerous and serious. My desperate struggles, on page 46 and in the foreword to the Second Impression, are worth recording for the *obiter dicta* about Rubinstein and Tchaikovsky which they occasion, but of course they do not attempt to excuse the slander and blunder the consequences of which they attempt to evade.

The footnote on page 47 states a mystery which I cannot attempt to explain. I am sure that Schumann would have scrupled to write such consecutive fifths if he had not echoed them; but why the echo remedies them I cannot think. Since it undoubtedly does, we need not worry.

Much new light has been thrown upon Bruckner by the recent

pious publication of his works in their original form as he conceived them before certain eminent conductors took them in hand.
Now this is not such a simple matter as it might seem. Bruckner
was an object of party warfare in his lifetime, a butt for the
'Brahminen', who saw no merit in him at all, a mascot for the
'Wagnerians', who had for the most part a poor grasp of instrumental music. The only musicians who had any chance of understanding Bruckner were the Wagnerians, who were, probably
without exception, violently opposed to Brahms, as Bruckner was
himself. And whatever the limitations, and however provocative
the arrogance of the Brahminen, there is no question that, except
in matters of theatre music, the deeper musical knowledge and
finer sensibilities were mainly on their side. To-day the pious
restoration of Bruckner's original form and scoring is acclaimed as
the restoration of things that were beyond the spiritual grasp of
the age, and particularly beyond the grasp of the great conductors
who made Bruckner's works practically possible by revising his
scoring and making cuts in his recapitulations and digressions. If
these changes had been made after Bruckner's death or against his
will, there would be a strong case for returning to his original
versions; but, apart from their intrinsic merits, they were all
accepted and published by him as expressing his final intentions.
And it is to these that piety is due.

   In future performances of Bruckner's works I shall certainly
profit by a close study of his original versions. But I do not expect
to find any reason, in piety to Bruckner, for rejecting the experience he accepted from Loewe. We are told that cuts were made
because the spirit of the age was not ripe for Bruckner. The
limitations of Bruckner's champions certainly did not include a
blindness to his spiritual qualities; on the contrary, an out-and-out
Brucknerite was, in his day as now, a person of slow intellectual
processes to whom subtleties were as unintelligible as they were to
Bruckner himself, and for whom Brahms's mind was eight times
too alert. We ought rather to expect to find them obtuse as to
much that we pride ourselves on appreciating. But the situation is
by no means that of the transformation of Mussorgsky's *Boris
Godunov* at the hands of Rimsky-Korsakov. Rimsky-Korsakov's
brilliant mastery was the perfect expression of a perky and con-
ceited little mind, which was no more capable of telling a blunder
from a stroke of genius or feature of style, than Herbert Spencer
was capable of producing an authoritative edition of Plato. Bruckner's champions were modest practical men, inspired conductors
worthy of the confidence Wagner showed in them; and Bruckner
did well to publish his works in the form in which these faithful
champions revised them. I cannot claim, as yet, to have made a

study of the evolution of Bruckner's scores; but I can already cite one obvious example showing both the futility of returning to the original and the advisability of knowing something about it. I quote with praise, on p. 74 of Vol. II, the 'flowing figure in muted violins' that weaves clouds of incense round the main theme on its return deepened in octaves. To an expert in orchestration it must seem incredible that this figure should have been entrusted merely to an unsupported flute; yet such is the case. The flute is still there in the revised version, but the weight of the tone, and all its security of legato, is in the muted violins. I have heard the 'Romantic' Symphony since the publication of the original score, and have noticed with pleasure that the conductor used the ordinary revised version but made the flute more prominent than usual, thus realizing the composer's first idea under the far better conditions of the revision, and incidentally showing how history repeats itself, since Haydn's orchestration shows frequent signs of the inability of his flutes to support themselves.

I should be very much surprised to find myself tempted to restore Bruckner's original complete recapitulations. The most *ungebildet* phenomenon in his treatment of form is his failure to see the irrelevance of his vestiges of classical procedure.

On page 124–5 I give, from personal information, the demand of Sibelius that the conductor should visibly change his beat according to the shifting accents. In common with other and perhaps more widely experienced conductors I find this unnecessary and confusing. In ordinary syncopations it is a fault if the conductor falls out of the normal beat. Sibelius's $\frac{6}{4}$ *versus* $\frac{3}{2}$ is not a case of syncopation: he wishes both forms of accent to be equally normal and hence desires the conductor to indicate the change. But sometimes the two rhythms are simultaneous, and in any case the conductor's efforts will fail to make the listener believe his eyes rather than his ears.

On page 146 I cite a record 'in Mendelssohn's letters' of a performance of the Scherzo of his Octet in church. I cannot trace this, and I may as well suppose that I have dreamt it.

Bach's C minor Double Concerto has recently been published restored for Violin and Oboe in D minor. Nevertheless, I remain convinced that C minor is the right key. The compass of the oboe would already make this probable, for D minor would take the oboe up to E, whereas D is Bach's inviolable limit for the instrument. But there is conclusive evidence for C minor in passages where the clavier faithfully records the fact that the violin substitutes its open G for the low F that would have resulted from an exact transposition of the figures as first given in a higher key.

Apropos of Handel's Hornpipes (page 201), I now finally yield to the temptation to quote the following spirited example, which ought to be found somewhere in the British Museum. (If not, I shall put it there myself.)

Volume III

An occasional feature in these essays is an attempt to present the facts so that listeners may enjoy the element of surprise where the composer so intends. Thus in Vol. III, p. 54, I have tried to leave the listener only half prepared for the solo violin's production of the opening 'trumpet' theme at the pitch of a piccolo.

As my addendum to the reprint of Vol. III shows, the Violoncello Concerto attributed to Haydn is by Anton Kraft, and will be found under that heading in the Index.

I am glad to hear that the title 'Emperor' for Beethoven's E flat Concerto is quite unknown in Germany.

The preface to the miniature score of Brahms's Violin Concerto gives many interesting particulars as to the genesis of that work. (But the English translation must first be translated back into German; it makes appalling blunders and implies that Brahms disapproved of Joachim's interpretation.)

I was at first inclined to be violently sceptical as to Dr. Altmann's suggestion that the rejected scherzo of the Violin Concerto may have become the tremendous second movement of the B flat Pianoforte Concerto. But sketches may advance a considerable way before they become too firmly set for drastic transformation. This is by no means an unlikely violin theme—

In the Violin Concerto, Ex. 6, p. 127, there is some reason to suspect an allusion, personal to Joachim and Brahms, to a prominent theme in Viotti's A minor Violin Concerto, a work of which both masters were specially fond (see the following example). With less probability, Viotti may be suspected of haunting Brahms with the rhythm of Ex. 2 in the Double Concerto (p. 141), but by this time the causal nexus is thinning out in uncontrolled diffusion, and might as well be extended to a similar figure in the first movement of the Clarinet Trio, Op. 114.

Volume IV

Here my troubles really begin. Evil communications corrupt good manners, and what I have called 'the encyclopædic inattention' of the gratuitously illustrative composer enwraps my mind in a fog of that kind of General Culture which is to be sharply and exclusively distinguished from musical culture. We cannot be too grateful to Elgar for his courtesy, so soon before he joined the ages, in allowing me to 'control' my analysis of that greatest of symphonic poems, *Falstaff*, by his own. Thus far I am protected. But Nemesis descends upon me with my footnote to page 77. Having fallen into the usual booby trap of the legend of Paganini's playing the viola part in Berlioz's *Harold* Symphony, I took an insolent pride in shifting my responsibility for the error upon Berlioz after having argued that his word was as the word of Baron Münchhausen. But on that argument the legend would be true, for Berlioz's word happens to be precisely the contrary: he tells us the truth, that Paganini not only commissioned the work but paid him generously for it, and heard its first performance but refused to play the viola part.

In answer to many friendly critics, and in defence of the printing-office proof-readers whose accuracy far transcends mine, I must point out that 'Phileas' Fogg is not a misprint. Jules Verne's 'Phileas' is one of the strongest of bilingual ties between England and France, worthy to be ranked with The First of the Fourth (*le premier du quatrième*), which Hugo persisted in believing to be our queer name for a certain Scottish estuary, his typical British Tar Mr. Tom-Tim-Jack, and the alias of the anarchist Ravachol when he passed as that eminent English man-about-town Mr. Flitpot.

I ought not to be surprised at the indignation aroused by my giving no authority for my statement, on page 82, that Berlioz coolly confessed that his famous story of Habeneck's inviting disaster by taking a pinch of snuff at a critical moment while conducting the *Grande Messe des Morts* was a fabrication told simply because it was *ben trovato*. (It certainly was not *ben trovato*; a more impossible story has never been told since Sir Boyle Roche wrote a letter with a pistol in each hand and a sword in the other.) This habit of quoting from memory will certainly get me into hot water some day. But my authority is first-rate, though I had forgotten it. The story was told to Sir Charles Stanford by J. A. Osborne and quoted in *Pages from an Unwritten Diary*, pp. 68–9.

I ought to have known all the time, instead of waiting till Vol. IV was reprinted, that the wonderful chord, Ex. 2, in Mendelssohn's Overture to *A Midsummer Night's Dream*, had already been written in 1790 by Mozart in *Così fan tutte*.

No light has yet reached me as to the 'well-known tune' concealed beneath the theme of Elgar's *Enigma* Variations. For some time the rumour was rife that the tune was *Auld Lang Syne*. It was not. We may be perfectly certain that whatever it was there would be nothing Straussian or archaic about the combination as counterpoint. With all his admiration for Strauss, Elgar is one of the cleanest contrapuntists in musical history. Road-hog counterpoint simply did not interest him; and, if it did, to make an enigma of road-hog counterpoint is merely to put 'barking like a dog' into a riddle about a partridge 'to make it harder'.

Alas and alack-a-day, Hindemith, in his new *Anweisungen zur Tonsatz*, expressly repudiates atonality and polytonality, in terms, which give no support to the idea that he ever used these privileges even in early works! Still, facts are facts; and while I apologize to the composer of Hindemith's Op. 24, No. 1, I see nothing to retract either in my account of that particular work or in my account of the hypotheses on which I now know that it is not constructed. Hindemith's development is rapid, and his practice as well as his theory has cleared up since 1921. Certainly it is a fact that Herr Wilm Wilm's fox-trot is in one of the twelve major keys, and that it is accompanied by simultaneous identical runs in each of the other eleven. Moreover, in rehearsing an early violin sonata with a great violinist I found it impossible at first to get good intonation for a passage in which the violin was on the top, the right hand of the pianoforte playing the same melody a major sixth below, and the left hand playing it another major sixth below the right. But, taking the tune at its face value, I found that it lent itself naturally to harmonization in terms of Spohr. Thus harmonized, the violinist read it easily at sight, and, having once learned it, did not forget it when it was doubled in two other keys. Be this as it may, Hindemith's later work is undoubtedly broadening its range and getting rid of *a priori* encumbrances.

Volume V

Apart from a misplaced bass clef, which made the 'rude Sylvanus' intrude too soon into the peace of Weelkes's *Three Virgin Nymphs*, the first and chief serious mistake is the wild statement that Brahms's *Deutsches Requiem* commemorated the fallen in the wars of 1870. The first three numbers of the *Requiem* were performed in 1867, the whole work, except for the soprano solo, in 1868; and the soprano solo commemorates not his step-mother, who died much later, but his mother, whose death in 1865 was presumably the occasion from which the whole *Requiem* originated.

Debussy did not submit his *Blessed Damozel* for the *Prix de Rome*. He had already won that prize with his cantata *L'Enfant Prodigue*. But when he did send *La Damoiselle Élue* from Rome, the Section des Beaux-Arts of the Institut rejected it. So the point I was trying to make is good enough for conversational purposes.

One or two anachronisms seem to have slipped in, rather from grammatical ambiguity than from real confusion. Loewe's *Erlkönig*, for instance, is only a year or two later than Schubert's: yet I still think his clever economy typical of the decline from a golden to a silver age. That is a golden age which is dominated by men of supreme genius, who are just as likely to put the clock back from an already tarnished silver age as to put it forward. At all events the preference for Loewe is a typical silver-age taste.

When I said that Parry and Stanford offended our professional librettists and critics by choosing their own words instead of leaving English choral music in that state of culture to which it had pleased Mr. Chorley to call it, I did not mean to imply that Chorley was a contemporary, nor had I any curiosity as to the date of his death, which I find to be 1872. The Chorleys we have always with us: like Herodotus, I know their names but forbear to mention them. Chorley was an honourable man. So are they all, all honourable men. Peace be to their waste-paper baskets and to mine.

GLOSSARY

THIS glossary does not attempt the hopeless task of making an equivalent of a systematic treatise out of the *disjecta membra* of which these six volumes consist: it merely explains such musical terms as I find I have used without the explanation that some of my most intelligent readers may be glad to have. To those who can read music much of this glossary may seem unnecessary, though not all its explanations are orthodox; but there are many persons highly gifted in musical sensibility to whom the information here given will at least explain the extent to which my terminology is Pickwickian.

ARPEGGIO

A chord of which the notes are delivered one after another, whether or not then sustained, and regardless of their order in succession. As the word implies, such chords are characteristic of the harp, on which instrument chords are most sonorous when the strings are plucked in rapid succession from the bass upwards instead of all exactly together.

ATONALITY

The art of composing not merely ambiguously as to key, or with change of key too constant to be followed, but actually in a style that excludes all association whatever with keys or tonality. Not to be confused with 'polytonality' (q.v.); though, like polytonality, it will probably prove to be, in all its forms, a mere contradiction in terms resulting from trying to make an abstraction out of a small number of special effects ultimately derived from classical music. (See also 'Whole-tone Scale'.) (See Essay No. cxcv, vol. iv, pp. 172–3. Analysis of Hindemith's *Kammermusik*, No. 1, op. 24, No. 1; but note that Hindemith expressly repudiates atonality and polytonality.)

AUGMENTATION

The delivery of a theme in notes systematically longer than those of the original; a device used primarily in fugues, though augmentations, both strict and free, are used as means of transformation or development in other compositions. Distinguish between genuine augmentation and the appearances of notation when a slow theme returns over accessories in quick tempo, as the Pilgrims' Chorus at the end of the Overture to *Tannhäuser*.

CEMBALO

For all practical purposes the reader may take this as meaning 'harpsichord'. The forms *Clavicembalo* and *Gravicembalo* **are** found.

CHACONNE

Originally a dance in rather slow triple time, with a strong accent on the second beat; closely allied to the 'passacaglia' (q.v.). It had a processional character which, like the passacaglia, made its music conveniently fall into a long series of variations (q.v.) on a single phrase. In the ballets of Gluck's operas the chaconne is no such series, but a long and freely developed symphonic movement in an energetic tempo of three in a bar.

CHROMATIC

A chromatic (i.e. 'coloured') scale is one that fills up the tones of the diatonic scale with semitones. Important matters of style depend on the harmonic meaning of such semitones. Their meaning may range from mere colourless inter-harmonic gliding to the profoundest and most iridescent ambiguities and paradoxes of Chopin and Wagner. Moreover, not everything that results in a chromatic scale is chromatic harmony. The following example is an entirely diatonic series of rapid changes of key (see 'Modulation'; and Introduction, on 'Tonality'):

A chord is chromatic only if, while foreign to the key in which it appears, it does not intend or imply a change of key. The simplest case of a chromatic chord is the supertonic triad or seventh with a major third, as in the following cadence in C major:

CLAVICHORD

The strings of the clavichord are not plucked by 'jacks' (plectrums) but set in vibration by 'tangents', upright metal laths, which are both the exciting cause of the sound and determinative of its pitch. The shorter portion of the string emerges from a wrapping of baize which permanently damps it. When the player puts down a key he thereby causes the tangent to press the string upwards. This pressure produces a musical note whose pitch depends on the length of the string between the tangent and the tuning-pin. It becomes sharper with increased pressure, and is capable of vibrato; emotional effects much esteemed and artistically used by the great musicians of the period. Thus the clavichord, though possessed of a very small tone unsuitable for display in a large room, is an extremely sensitive and suggestive instrument. See also 'Clavier'. Certain features of style in *Das Wohltemperirte Clavier* lead to the inference that Bach is often thinking of the clavichord rather than the harpsichord. But this is not an ascertainable matter. Composers did not limit the circulation of their clavier works by too precisely specifying what clavier they intended. They were as practical as the modern publisher who pointed out that the nobly alliterative title *The Bad Boy's Book of Beasts* would necessarily have only half the selling power of *The Bad Child's Book of Beasts*. In any case the conscientious editor who translates Bach's title as *The Well-tempered Clavichord* commits the mistake of attributing too precise a temperament to an instrument whose unison-strings were always tuned slightly at variance (like the voix celeste of the organ) in order to make the tiny tone more penetrating and expressive.

CLAVIER

Generic term, up to the middle of the eighteenth century, for keyboard instruments, including the manuals of the organ. Thus it comprises the 'clavichord' (q.v.), the 'harpsichord' (q.v.), and the harpsichord's ancestral and diminutive forms, the virginals and spinet.

COMMON CHORDS

Common chords are 'triads' (q.v.) of which the 5th is perfect and the 3rd major or minor. Doublings and dispersal through various octaves are ignored so long as the 'root' (q.v.) is in the bass. They are concords, and every normal piece of classical music closes on a complete or implied major or minor tonic common chord; a bare 5th, 8ve, or unison, being the skeleton of such a chord. (See Introduction on 'Tonality' (vol. i, pp. 7–9).)

CONCORD, CONSONANCE: DISCORD, DISSONANCE

Concord and discord are relative terms signifying opposite differences of degree in resonance, relevance, and finality. The literary uses of these terms make it advisable to warn the general reader that in musical parlance the terms are grammatical as well as relative. The musician knows what the non-musician means by complaining that such and such a music is 'full of discords'; but, strictly speaking, one might as well complain that a narrative was full of transitive verbs. It is only in an almost pre-harmonic state of music that pure acoustic smoothness is the main criterion of concord. When classical poets speak of 'symphony' and 'perfect diapason' they imply (purposely or unintentionally) unison and octaves. (See vol. v, Essay CCXVIII, p. 232, analysis of Parry's *Blest Pair of Sirens*.) The 'perfect concords' (4ths, 5ths, and 8ves) have, in classical harmony (including counterpoint), so elementary a resonance that many restrictions govern their consecutive use between any two parts of the harmony lest false resonances and hollows result. The 'imperfect concords' were considered discords in the twelfth century, before counterpoint was evolved. In classical music no harmony is complete without them, and on them depends the distinction between minor and major modes. (See Introduction on 'Tonality'.) Moreover, a chord without dissonance in itself may become grammatically discordant in an unexpected context. In such cases it would make no grammatical difference if actual dissonances from the context were introduced into the chord. Many of Wagner's discords that most shocked his contemporaries are thus acoustically less harsh than some of the most familiar classical chords.

(See also 'Preparation' (*a*); 'Resolution'; 'Suspension'; 'Passing-note'; 'Essential'.)

CONJUNCT MOTION (movement).
See 'Motion'.

CONTRAPUNTAL
The adjective of 'Counterpoint' (q.v.).

CONTRARY MOTION (movement).
See 'Motion'.

COUNTERPOINT
'Point counter point', i.e. 'note against note'; the art of making harmony by means of a combination of melodies. Ouseley's famous definition, 'the art of combining melodies', is inadequate, and applies better to the primitive efforts from which counterpoint (and hence harmony) arose; the simultaneous singing of pre-existing melodies with rough-hewing to get rid of the worst discords. (See vol. iv, pp. 126–7, analysis of *Vorspiel* to *Meistersinger*.) Counterpoint is a general category of music, best understood as the origin of most of the classical grammar of harmony, and as comprising *polyphony*, which is implicitly limited to the case of textures in which all parts are of more or less equal value.

COUNTER-STATEMENT
A restatement immediately following the original statement and turned in another direction. Distinguish from *Recapitulation*, *Variation*, and mere repetition.

COUNTER-SUBJECT

A theme consistently maintained as a counterpoint combined with the main subject of a fugue. The use of this term is normally restricted to the case of a recognizable theme systematically used as counterpoint to the *subject* of a fugue. (For 'Fugue' see Introduction, vol. i, pp. 17 ff.) The counter-subject normally first appears as the accompaniment furnished to the Answer by the part which announced the Subject. Counter-subjects that first appear later in a fugue become so conspicuous from the delay that they earn the courtesy title of second subjects, though Cherubini, for obscure reasons of discipline, deals harshly with such pretensions.

DEUX-TEMPS

A waltz-rhythm in which the melody floats in a pattern of thrice two ($1 2$ $3 4$ $5 6$) over the ordinary waltz basis of thrice three ($1 2 3$ $4 5 6$). The waltz in Gounod's *Faust* is a deux-temps ($\frac{3}{4}$ ♩ ♪ ♩ | ♪ ♩. ♪♩ ♩ ♪ ♩ ♪). The cross-rhythm of $\frac{2}{4}$ over $\frac{3}{4}$, as in Chopin's Waltz, op. 42, is another matter, beyond the range of ordinary dance-music.

DEVELOPMENT

(*a*) The breaking up of themes and recombining their portions (figures, q.v.) into new phrases and sequences (q.v.). (*b*) The section specially devoted to such processes (sometimes called 'working out' or 'free fantasia') in the middle of a 'movement' (q.v.). Distinguish from *Variation* and the devices specially applied to the subjects of fugues.

DIATONIC

A scientific definition of the diatonic scale is beyond the scope of these essays, if, indeed, it has yet been achieved to the satisfaction of musicians and men of science. The reader may therefore rest for the present contented with his familiar notion of the scale approximately produced by the white keys of the pianoforte, and transposable to other pitches by apt use of the black keys. This notion, however, should not be confined to the scale typified by C major (otherwise the Ionian Mode), but should include all the other Church Modes as producible by the white keys; the Dorian, from D to D; Phrygian, from E to E; Lydian, from F to F; Mixolydian, from G to G; and Aeolian, from A to A. Moreover, we should realize that good choirs, and also good string-quartet players, when left to their own instincts without the accompaniment of pianoforte or organ, will produce diatonic music in 'just intonation', with a precision, and a consequent euphony, far beyond reach of any instrument with a number of notes limited, and therefore 'tempered' in their tuning, by practical necessity. (See 'Chromatic', 'Temperament', and 'Enharmonic'.)

DIMINUTION

The opposite of 'Augmentation' (q.v.), i.e. the delivery of a theme in notes systematically shorter than those of the original.

DISCORD, DISSONANCE

See 'Concord'.

DOUBLE COUNTERPOINT, TRIPLE COUNTERPOINT, &c.

To the explanation given under 'Inversion' (b) it remains to add that combinations may be so devised that one (or in rare cases more) of the melodies may be transposed by some other interval than the octave relatively to the others. In the case of Double Counterpoint in the 12th this gives rise to new harmonies and a new tonal orientation (see Brahms, *Variations on a Theme of Hadyn*, Essay LXI, vol. ii, p. 138). With Double Counterpoint in the 10th it makes numerous doublings and interlockings in 3rds and 6ths possible.

ENHARMONIC

An enharmonic modulation is one which changes the intonation of part of a chord by a quantity inexpressible on keyboard instruments (as from C♯ to D♭), and then treats the chord in its new sense. Not everything that looks enharmonic on paper is so in reality: convenience or caprice of notation may make a simple diatonic change seem enharmonic, when mere transposition to a key where the complex notation becomes inconvenient will cause the enharmonic semblance to vanish. (See Essay XLVII, on Beethoven's Ninth Symphony, vol. ii, p. 15, Ex. 6, with remarks on the parallel passages, pp. 19–20.)

An enharmonic circle is a series of keys that returns to its starting-point on tempered instruments, but in mathematically ideal intonation fails to do so by an enharmonic quantity. Thus the finale of Beethoven's Sonata, op. 54, goes right round the 'circle of 5ths', the longest possible of enharmonic circles; and the first movement of Brahms's Third Symphony goes several times round a circle of major 3rds (F, D♭, B♭♭ = A, F). The same circle is shown in the four movements of his First Symphony, moving in the opposite direction (C minor, E major, G♯ major = A♭, C major). Another case is that of Schumann's first Novelette.

There is a widespread, but totally wrong, idea that enharmonic modulations depend on the tempered scale. They were explored by one of the greatest masters of the Golden Age, Marenzio, long before singers dreamt of singing in anything but 'just intonation';

and they mean exactly the same on keyboard instruments, that cannot express their actuality, as they mean on voices and stringed instruments that can. The musical ear has no more difficulty in understanding their meaning as implied on the keyboard than the linguistic ear has in ignoring the phonetic inaccuracy of a pun.

EPISODE

Generally any fairly definite section separating the main themes, or interpolated into the development of a composition. More specially:

(*a*) Those passages in a fugue which separate one completed entry of the subject from another entry after an appreciable interval. Such passages do not interrupt the flow, and they develop previous material rather than displaying independence.

(*b*) A new theme appearing in the course of the development of a movement in sonata form: e.g. the E minor theme in the first movement of the Eroica Symphony (Essay IV, vol. i, pp. 29 ff., Ex. 3). Some teachers, deeply committed to the terms First Subject and Second Subject, apply the term Episode to passages in the exposition of a sonata-form movement lying between the theme they call Second Subject and the closing theme or cadence-theme. This throws upon the analyst the vexatious task of deciding in compositions like the Eroica Symphony, which of half a dozen themes is worthiest to be called the Second Subject. (See 'Subject' and Introduction on Sonata form.)

(*c*) The episodes of a Rondo (see Introduction) are the more or less well defined and important sections which separate the recurrences of the rondo-theme.

ESSENTIAL DISCORDS

Essential discords are discords which have become established in their own right as secondary only to *common chords*. They are practically all ultimately referable to the dominant (see 'Tonality' in Introduction) and there is no clear borderline between essential and unessential. No discord was thought of as essential until the Monodic revolution (see 'Monody') had done its work.

FIGURE (German: *MOTIF*)

The smallest recognizable fragment broken off from a theme. In mature Wagnerian opera every theme and every figure naturally becomes a dramatic symbol of the situation and words with which it was first associated; and the fascinating and easy analysis of the resultant *Leitmotive* has greatly promoted the doctrine, against which my essays constantly protest, that good music is *built up* from small figures, instead of consisting of larger things from which small figures can be broken off.

FIGURED BASS or CONTINUO

A bass part for the use of the organist or cembalist (harpsi-chordist) in music between *c.* 1600 and the Church music of Mozart, indicating by numeral figures the chords of the harmony to be filled in at the keyboard.

FUGATO

A passage in the style of a fugue. (For 'Fugue' see Introductory Essay, vol. i.)

FUNDAMENTAL BASS

A bass, imaginary except in so far as coinciding with the actual bass, consisting entirely of the 'roots' (q.v.) of the harmony. The theory of the Fundamental Bass (with the term itself) was worked out by Rameau (1683–1764) and had its use in giving students a more definite notion of chords and tonality than could be obtained from purely contrapuntal principles. But Philipp Emanuel Bach already saw its limitations when he remarked to Burney that it childishly reduced all music to a series of full closes; and it did in fact lead to the worst rigidities and complexities of the teaching of harmony in the nineteenth century. These are more or less like analysing language without understanding the uses of meta-phor, and most typically, without understanding how much of current English is metaphorical as compared with classical Greek prose.

HARMONICS

Overtones in the 'harmonic series' (q.v.) producible by varied lip pressure in the tubes of 'brass' instruments, and by touching a string at a point corresponding to a harmonic segment, lightly so as not to check the vibration of the whole string. Until valves were applied to trumpets and horns, so as to provide instant changes in the length of the tube, these instruments could produce only the notes of a single harmonic series, except the muffled 'closed' notes producible in the horn by blocking part of the bell with the hand.

HARMONIC SERIES

The natural series of overtones, or upper partials, corresponding in ratio to the harmonic progression $1.\frac{1}{2}.\frac{1}{3}.\frac{1}{4}$, &c. The first sixteen, reckoned from the open C string of a violoncello, are as follows:

$$1 \quad 2 \quad 3 \quad 4 \quad 5 \quad 6 \; \sharp 7 \quad 8 \quad 9 \quad 10 \; \sharp 11 \quad 12 \; \sharp 13 \; \sharp 14 \quad 15 \quad 16$$

No. 7 is so flat as not to lie within the scales of classical harmony at all. Probably the fashion (now become banal) of corrupting triads with an ungrammatical 'added 6th' is an unconscious striving to represent this flat 7th. The difference between the ratios 8–9 and 9–10 asserts itself wherever singers and string-players produce pure polyphony without accompaniment. No. 11 is another note outside classical harmony, and so is No. 13. No. 14 is, of course, the octave of No. 7. Nos. 15 and 16, on the other hand, give a perfectly classical diatonic semitone. The intervals between successive higher numbers, of course, continue to diminish, and so pass out of classical reckoning except for the octaves of the classical notes. The folly is manifest which would seek to derive all the phenomena of classical music from a natural series which already contradicts classical harmony after its first six terms. On the other hand, there is no sanity in a scepticism which would deny the musical relevance of those six.

HARPSICHORD

The strings of the harpsichord, virginals, and spinet are plucked by 'jacks', upright carriers of horizontal spines of raven-quill operated by the keys under the player's hands. (Nobody knows what Shakespeare means by describing the jacks as kissing the palms of his lady's hands; they are as obviously incapable of this as the hammers of the pianoforte; and it is no less inconceivable that Shakespeare's meaning can be the nonsense that it seems to be.) Large harpsichords have several sets of jacks and several sets of strings, including octave strings above and below the central pitch, and also furnishing decided contrasts of tone-colour according to the position and nature of the plectrum. (The position does not affect the pitch, as in the clavichord, for the whole string vibrates.) Besides these resources large harpsichords have two keyboards. Composers were, nevertheless, careful not to limit the circulation of their works by often writing intricacies impossible on one keyboard. Only three of Bach's clavier works explicitly demand simultaneous contrasts of tone, and only one of these three contains passages otherwise too involved for one keyboard.

Thus the harpsichord has a large variety of contrasted tone-colours, six distinct combinations being implicit in the lay-out of Bach's *Italian Concerto* and *French Overture*. On the other hand, it lacks the subtle nuances directly controlled by the fingers of the clavichord-player (see 'Clavichord').

HOMOPHONY; HOMOPHONIC

Music that avoids all appearance of its opposite, *polyphony* (see 'Counterpoint'), expressing its harmony in terms of chords simply massed, broken (see 'Arpeggio'), or repeated in rhythmic formulas. Not coextensive with 'Monody' (q.v.).

IMITATION

Free and sporadic *canon*, i.e. the imitating of one voice by one or more others at short time-intervals so that the voices overlap. *Canon* is strict and continuous imitation, *sc.* relation of one part to another by a rigid rule; the actual 'canon' being, in early examples, the rule by which the unwritten follower was to be deduced from the leader; e.g. 'I give tithes of all I possess' indicating canon in the 10th; and 'Get thee behind me, Satan' (*Vade retro*) indicating that the answering voice should sing backwards.

INTERVAL

The musical sense of this word applies only to the pitch-relations of notes. As a rule, care is taken in these essays to avoid using musical terms in any non-musical sense that they may have in ordinary language, except in cases where the author fails to suspect any source of confusion. Experience shows that the word 'interval' can cause confusion to general readers who take considerable trouble to inquire into musical matters. An exact grammatical article on intervals, however necessary for students, is not to the purpose of these volumes: but I have known Balliol scholars to waste labour on Greek music from not knowing that our names of intervals do not denote fractions but are the results of counting the steps of a scale from the bottom note of the interval to its top, both inclusively; thus the 5th from C is G, because C and G are boundaries of five notes of the scale (C,D,E,F,G). Many translations of musical treatises teem with blunders on these points. There is an old English version of Jean-Jacques Rousseau's *Musical Dictionary* which must be translated back into French before you can be sure whether '5th' means ⅝, No. 5, or the viola! It seldom seems to mean the interval.

INTONATION

1. (*a*) Tuning (see 'Just Intonation'); (*b*) the art of singing or playing in tune. 2. Any piece of Gregorian or Ambrosian or Anglican chant (including monotone) as delivered by a single voice.

INVERSION

(*a*) The more or less exact reversal of the rise and fall of the notes of a melody (e.g. several cases in Brahms's First Symphony; see Essay XI, vol. i, pp. 84 ff., Exx. 7, 10, 16, 23).

(*b*) The inversions of Double (and Triple, &c.) Counterpoint (q.v.) are the permutations of its possible positions.

(*c*) A chord is inverted when its root is not in the bass; thus a common chord has two inversions:

Root position.   1st inversion.   2nd inversion.

JUST INTONATION

Performing in tune with a mathematical precision according to what classical harmony implies. Voices, instruments of the violin tribe, and slide trombones can approximate to this, since they make their own notes with continuous graduation. Hence, as they can perform indefinitely out of tune, so they can perform in better tune than keyed instruments with a limited number of notes. What degree of mathematical precision classical harmony implies, where it implies it, and what harmony is classical, are questions which science will not answer in haste. But the experience of unaccompanied (and uncorrupted) choirs and first-rate string-quartet players shows that just intonation does exist, under certain favourable conditions. (See 'Temperament'.)

MARKS OF EXPRESSION

The reader will need no information about the commoner marks of expression and their abbreviations; but certain distinctions are worth noting. Whereas *fp* means *forte-piano*, i.e. a loud note suddenly damped to softness, *pf* does not mean the opposite process (an effect in any case difficult to make convincing) but stands for *poco forte*, just as *mf* stands for *mezzo-forte*.

Distinguish between *sf*, *sforzando*, a sharp accent on a single note, and *rf*, *rinforzando*, a sudden reinforcement maintained at a level presumably until the next indication.

Dim. for *diminuendo* is used by Beethoven and most composers as the opposite of *crescendo*. But some connect it also with a slackening of time; notably Schubert, who often follows it by *a tempo*, having previously used no such sign as *rall.* (*rallentando*) or *rit.* (*ritardando*). With this possibility the word *decrescendo* is less ambiguous. But if composers adopt the picturesque habit of spreading a *cres - - - - cen - - - - do - - - -* thus over several lines, they must not blame the printers if the turn of a line or a page produces disaster to a *de - - - - cres - - - - cen - - - - do - - - -*.

MODULATION

The general reader may need warning that in music the word modulation means change of key and nothing else. Even the modulations of the Church Modes, which are simply the privileges of making full closes on chords based elsewhere than on the final of the mode, differ from changes of key only in degree, in so far as the modal composer never thought of 'establishing' a key. The ordinary use of the word, as when we speak of a beautifully modulated voice, must be allowed its actual precedence over the musical sense. Contrast the case of 'tonality' (see Introduction, Vol. I, on that subject), a word which has never had any but a musical sense. One of our most famous novelists, who often says good things about music, and who has more than once remarked upon the pitfalls which it prepares for the the unwary conversationalist, has represented some musicians as discussing a young player's tonality. They might have discussed his tone, or even his capacity for modulating his tone; but they ought never to have used the word 'tonality' of anything but the work of a composer.

MONODY

The art by which the Monodists (Peri, Cavalieri, Monteverdi, &c.) at the outset of the seventeenth century laid the foundations of opera, oratorio, and (incidentally) instrumental music: the development of dramatic and lyric singing by one voice over an instrumental accompaniment of homophonic chords. Thus not coextensive with 'Homophony' (q.v.).

MOTION (or *Movement* (c)).

The rise and fall of two parts relatively to each other is obviously classified into three kinds of *motion*, or movement.

In *Contrary* motion one part rises while the other falls. In *Similar* motion both parts move in the same direction, though not necessarily to the same extent. In *Oblique* motion one part moves while the other stands still. The term *Parallel* motion has been applied (perhaps first by some Irish school of theorists, or by the drivers of colliding motors) to the condition where neither part moves.

Contrary motion is an element of safety as well as of variety in harmony and counterpoint. Not only does it tend to resolve most discords (see 'Discord' and 'Resolution') but it explains away many otherwise unclassifiable discords and reduces their harshness often to imperceptibility. Most errors in harmony and counterpoint occur only in similar motion, which, as such, can be neither blamed nor avoided, since up and down are the only ways in which parts can move, so that with more than two moving parts some must be in similar motion. Polyphony cannot always fly for safety to oblique motion.

Conjunct movement (here 'movement' is more usual than 'motion') is the movement of any part by degrees of a scale without skips. This is what Grove means by saying that many of

Beethoven's melodies consist largely of 'consecutive notes'—a statement that has puzzled many readers who cannot see how a sentence could fail to consist, not only largely but entirely, of consecutive syllables.

MOVEMENT

(*a*) Used in the ordinary significance of the word; the sense of movement being a fundamental element in music, and one in which the great composers are strongest, as the small composers are weakest.

(*b*) In the technical musical sense a movement is a complete self-contained part of a larger composition, needing other movements to complement its emotional effect, but not needing them to complete its form or its treatment of its themes. Any allusion by one movement to the themes of a former one is thus an allusion to a finished past. The tempo of a classical movement is either fixed or subject only to changes which alternate in a simple and symmetrical way.

(*c*) The relative movement of parts: see 'Motion'.

OBLIQUE MOTION (or *Movement*).
See 'Motion'.

PASSING NOTES

Dissonant notes, usually on unaccented moments of rhythm, normally passing up and down the scale between concordant notes. They are the most 'unessential' of discords. Passing notes by skip are possible, in a complex musical language. See the Andante of Mozart's E flat Symphony; Essay XXIII, vol. i, pp. 189-90. (See 'Essential Discords'.)

PEDAL

(*a*) A note, normally in the bass and either the tonic or dominant, sustained immovably through harmonies that proceed regardless of conflict with it. (It is not worth calling a pedal if it is merely a normal component of the harmonies.) A pedal-note elsewhere than in the bass is called an inverted pedal. Another term for a pedal is *organ-point*; but readers should be warned that the French expression *point-d'orgue* means any kind of sustained pause, such as is expressed by the sign ⌒ over a chord or note.

(*b*) The pedal notes of certain brass instruments (especially trombones) are the fundamental notes of the tube, obtained with some difficulty by a specially loose lip and a great quantity of breath.

(*c*) The seven pedals of the harp convert its scale one by one, in two stages, from the diatonic scale of C♭ to all other scales up to C♯, and hence give it command of the chromatic intervals with possibilities restricted by the agility of two human feet.

The reader presumably needs no information about the pedals of the pianoforte and the organ.

POLYTONALITY

Not the mixing of several keys in a harmonic scheme, but the writing of several parts (whether independent or duplicates of each other) each in its own different key. As with 'Atonality' and the 'Whole-tone Scale' (q.v.), the listener will do well to enjoy without prejudice the pleasure which the masterly handling of these devices can give, without committing himself to a belief in the official theories of their propagandists, who are often weak and superficial in their efforts to relate and contrast the new theories with classical practice. (See Hindemith, Chamber Music No. 1, op. 24, no. 1, Essay CXCV, vol. iv, pp. 172–3.)

PREPARATION

(a) A discord is said to be prepared when the dissonant note has first been heard as part of a concord, and becomes a discord by being retained while the rest of the harmony changes.

(b) *Dominant preparation* is the emphatic and formal establishment of a key by harping on its dominant before settling down to a main theme or other event in that key. (See Introduction, on 'Tonality'.)

RECAPITULATION

Repetition of one or more large groups of material, usually after intermediate developments or episodes, and turned in the direction of finality.

RECITATIVE

Musical declamation governed entirely by speech-rhythm, and accordingly absolved from fixed 'tempo' (q.v.) and conforming with a time-signature (see 'Time') only by a convention of notation.

RESOLUTION

The completion of the sense of a discord by making the dissonant voice proceed with melodic logic to a concord. The smoothest and most normal resolutions are by a step down one degree of the scale. Upward resolutions and resolutions by skip are usually harsher and often imply some ellipsis or circumlocution. If a discord is compared with a transitive verb, preparation would be its subject and resolution its object. Most of the more complex associated phenomena develop in music in much the same way as in language.

ROOT

That note of a chord from which, if it is placed in the bass, the rest of the chord is seen to arise wholly or in great part as 'essential' (q.v.), consisting mainly of a common chord or a dominant discord. (See Introduction on 'Tonality', vol. i, p. 7; example giving the common chords in the key of C major. See also 'Fundamental Bass'.)

SEQUENCE

Repetitions of a 'figure' (q.v.) whether in melody alone or also in harmony, on different degrees of a scale. The second part of 'God save the King' ('Send him victorious, Happy and glorious') shows two steps in sequence in the melody, and also shows that these require a somewhat different sequence in their bass.

When, as in this and most melodic examples, the figure is warped by its changes of position within the same scale, the sequence is *tonal*. When the figure is exactly transposed, changing its key at each step, the sequence is *real*. Thus in Beethoven's Waldstein Sonata, op. 53, bars 5–8 repeat bars 1–4 in real sequence. Some 40 bars before the end the same figures, with brilliant counterpoints, are developed in tonal sequence with powerful rhetorical effect highly characteristic of perorations in which topics, at first separated, have become concentrated into one key.

SIMILAR MOTION (or *Movement*).

See 'Motion'.

STRINGENDO

= pulling together. It is purely an indication of time-hurrying, perhaps more intense than *accelerando*; whereas its cognate 'stretto' is almost exclusively used as a term of musical form. (See Introduction, vol. I, on 'Fugue'.)

SUBJECT

A term the musical uses of which are deplorably confused. (*a*) The subject of a fugue is its theme (see Introduction to vol. i under 'Fugue', where also the fugal sense of *Answer* is described). (*b*) The two main groups of material in the exposition of a sonata-form of movement are usually called *First Subject* and *Second Subject*. I regret that most of my analytical essays were written before I had hit upon the terms *First Group* and *Second Group* for such aggregates. (See Introduction to vol. i, pp. 11–12. Also see 'Counter-subject'.)

SUSPENSIONS

The typical case of prepared discords (see 'Preparation'), the suspended note being actually tied over from its previous concordant existence till it becomes an accented (but unessential) discord. Such a tied note is not a suspension if it produces an essential discord that must resolve on another chord, as in the following example of the preparation and resolution of a dominant 7th (an essential discord).

Ex. 1.

A true suspension requires no new chord on which to resolve but is merely a delay in the arrival of part of the chord over which it is suspended. Thus Ex. 1 will become a suspension if the lower parts remain as part of an E minor chord.

Ex. 2.

Example 3 is a true suspension—

Ex. 3.

and remains a true suspension even if the bass move to form another chord, since the suspended 9th has no more 'essential' meaning in any case.

Ex. 4.

TEMPERAMENT

Instruments whose notes are limited in number and rigidly tuned must represent the infinite mathematical complexities of harmony by striking such an average in the tuning of their notes as may give tolerable approximations to the greatest number of harmonic facts. Until the example set by *Das Wohltemperirte Clavier* of J. S. Bach was followed, systems of unequal temperament were used, by which the keys easiest for most orchestral instruments were tuned as well as possible at the expense of the rest. Bach's equal temperament, dividing the 8ve into twelve equal semitones (each in the ratio of $^{12}\sqrt{2}$), secured tolerable intonation for all keys, at a slight sacrifice in the tuning of the hitherto most favoured keys; and so gave the keyboard instruments freedom over all harmonic ranges. But it is a fundamental mistake to suppose that this was the means by which he created new harmonic values.

TEMPO

A uniform rate of rhythmic units. The classical Italian tempi may be ranged in the following order. The literal meanings of the words have for the most part ceased to have any relation to the mood of the music, except in the case of earlier composers.

Very slow tempi: *Grave* (lit. 'heavy', 'solemn'). *Largo* ('broad'). *Larghetto* (less broad than largo). *Adagio* ('at leisure').

Moderately slow tempi: *Andante* ('at a walking pace'). The diminutive *Andantino* should mean at a slower walk than *Andante*. See Beethoven's effort, in his Sonata, op. 109, Variation 4, to correct the already current mistake as to the meaning of *meno andante*. *Moderato* and *Allegretto* are not easily distinguished from *Andante con moto*.

Quick tempi: *Allegro* ('cheerful') is merely the average quick tempo and implies nothing as to mood. Handel, however, still means by *Andante allegro* 'going cheerfully'. *Vivace* ('lively') is quicker than allegro; and so we end with *Presto* and *Prestissimo*. Schumann, however, goes further, both in German and Italian; and in two of his works, having started *presto possibile*, indicates *più presto*.

THEME

(*a*) A single musical statement recognizable apart from its original context and capable of maintaining its identity through processes of development and transformation. There is no reason to seek a means of rigidly defining the length of a theme or delimiting it from its neighbours.

(*b*) The theme of a set of 'Variations' (q.v.) is normally a complete melody. In the case of a 'Passacaglia' (q.v.) or *Chaconne*, it is a single phrase of not more than eight bars, usually placed as a 'Ground-Bass' (q.v.). But see analysis of Brahms's Fourth Symphony (Essay XIV, vol. i, pp. 115 ff.) for a description of a passacaglia with its theme announced in the treble. Most variations are built on themes of more than one phrase, constituting complete tunes in one of the so-called binary and ternary forms (see Introduction, vol. i) with repeated sections. See also 'Figure', 'Subject'.

TIME

The regular grouping of rhythmic units, preserved under all changes of the audible rhythm. Thus, triple time is that in which the regular counting of rhythmic units by threes will keep every note of every part in place, whatever its length. The normal series of note-values is graded by subdivision into two, the semibreve being divided into two minims, the minim into two crotchets, the crotchet into two quavers, &c. Time-signatures resemble fractions of which the numerator shows the group and the denominator the note-value of the unit: thus $\frac{2}{4}$, $\frac{3}{4}$ (two crotchets; three crotchets). Normal subdivision of the units is ignored, however slow the tempo and however large the resulting unit, though if the units are permanently divided by three the time is called *compound* and the triplet notes are designated as the units. Thus $\frac{6}{8}$ is not a slow form of $\frac{3}{4}$ but is a duple time of two *dotted* crotchets each containing three quavers.

For historic reasons $\frac{2}{2}$ is represented by ₵ and is called *alla breve* time, and $\frac{4}{4}$ (or common time) is represented by C. These signs stand for the ancient semicircle indicating 'imperfect' time, so distinguished from the full circle indicating 'perfect' or triple time.

TRIAD

Any combination of a note with its 3rd and 5th. If the 5th is (*a*) imperfect, or (*b*) augmented, the triad is named accordingly

(*a*)   (*b*)

and is a discord. If either of the thirds is diminished the combina-

tion is not a triad at all but part of some more complex chord or progression. Concordant triads are *Common chords* (q.v.).

VARIATION

Applied in music to the transformation of a complete phrase or melody, preserving its integrity as a whole, whether the essential whole be conceived as melody, bass, harmony, or rhythmic scheme. Distinguish from *Development*.

WHOLE-TONE SCALE

A scale purporting to proceed in the whole tones of instruments tuned by equal temperament. It has undoubtedly been discovered in the course of extemporizing on such instruments; and before those who use it become tired of it they may believe that it and other phenomena of modern harmony are founded on the equally tempered scale. This is like supposing that geometry is founded on the carpenter's inability to make a microscopic approximation to incommensurable quantities. To the charge that the whole-tone scale is an impossible monstrosity the obvious replies are *solvitur ambulando*, and that it is vain to confront the giraffe with the assertion that 'there ain't no such animal'. But extravagant claims for the importance of the whole-tone scale are confronted by the fact that even in the too short career of its greatest master, Debussy, it represents a middle (though important) phase by no means co-extensive with his style, and that in his last works it tends to cede more place to other resources. At all times its charm depends on the fact that it really has an enharmonic kink—

$$\left(C \ D \ E \ \begin{Bmatrix} F\sharp \\ G\flat \end{Bmatrix} \begin{Bmatrix} G\sharp \\ A\flat \end{Bmatrix} \begin{Bmatrix} B\flat \\ A\sharp \end{Bmatrix} \begin{Bmatrix} C \\ B\sharp \end{Bmatrix} \right)$$

which becomes the more obvious with every effort to ignore it. Recently Walford Davies and others have shown that it is really a complicated chord projected into one octave. As such its absorption into the scheme of classical polyphony is inevitable as soon as that system is rediscovered.

Here are the six possible enharmonic variants of Holst's 'Word of wisdom' (vol. v, p. 256) in a position of an extended chord. This is neither better nor worse than other paradigms of harmonic possibilities: it is strictly grammatical according to classical practice, and, while no spontaneous composer would write so schematic a passage, all the six progressions are equally likely to pass unnoticed in Wagner or Brahms. It is a mere accident if they have not occurred before; and if you enjoy exploring haystacks for needles you may amuse yourself with seeking for these six progressions in *Tristan* and *Parsifal*. You are more likely to find each chord collapsing on the same augmented triad (F♯ B♭ D) in various spellings.

INDEX

This index relates to all the six volumes of
Essays in Musical Analysis. Those works to
which a complete essay is devoted have their
titles printed in small capital letters.

INDEX